TEXAS ON STAMPS

Texas on Stamps

By Jon L. Allen

Texas
Christian
University
Press

Library of Congress Cataloging-in-Publication

Allen, Jon L.
   Texas on Stamps / by Jon L. Allen
      p. cm.
   ISBN 0-87565-164-X (paper : alk. paper)
   1. Texas—On postage stamps—Catalogs. I. Title
HE6183. T44A43 1996
769.56′49764—dc20   96-14898
                                               CIP

Design by Shadetree Studio

By the same author
Stamp Collector's Guide to Europe
Aviation and Space Museums of America

FOREWORD

It didn't take long after the issuance of the first postage stamps in May 1840 for them to become collectibles. The world's first stamp was Great Britain's renowned Penny Black, bearing a likeness of Queen Victoria in profile. It was released on May 6, with a similar two-pence denomination released the following day.

France and Belgium issued their first postage stamps in 1849, then Spain and Switzerland in 1850 and other European nations during the next five years.

The United States, however, acted even more swiftly, recognizing the value of the adhesive postage stamp as a way to prepay charges. This country's first stamps were released on July 1, 1847. A five-cent denomination bore a likeness of Benjamin Franklin, while the ten cent featured a portrait of George Washington.

For half a century after 1840, most stamps depicted reigning monarchs or, in the case of the United States, former presidents. Then, by the turn of the century, several nations, among them the United States, began issuing stamps which were soon referred to as pictorials. They depicted ships, buildings, monuments, historic events, maps, castles and government buildings. Within a few years, pictorials featured scientists, musicians, artists, soldiers and, more recently, astronauts and cosmonauts, as well as animals, flowers, automobiles and even stamps on stamps.

A new field had been established for collectors. Rather than collecting by countries, many formed collections based on what was depicted on stamps, regardless of where they were issued.

Stamp collecting or philately, as it is formally known, became the world's most popular hobby early in the twentieth century. Inevitably, postal administrations recognized a vast potential market for issues, some never likely to be used, and young collectors soon became familiar with not only major nations of the world but also smaller states which printed stamps as a source of revenue. This practice has not abated but has, rather, increased as more and more states attained independence. Smaller states lacking the ability to design and print pictorial stamps rely upon foreign agencies for their production, as well as advice on topics likely to be in demand.

Early on, collectors started to form clubs and societies. Several of these were established in Europe quite early, and the oldest and largest such organization in the United States, the American Philatelic Society (APS), was incorporated in September 1886. Today, the APS has more than 56,000 members.

Texans were not far behind. A Texas Philatelic Association (TPA) was first proposed in San Antonio on October 1, 1896. Once the first twenty-five people had expressed interest in joining, a permanent organization was formed, officers elected and an official bulletin started.

The TPA held its first annual convention in San Antonio on April 21, 1897. The organization now has some thirty chapters throughout the state.

Moreover, two excellent philatelic research libraries are located in the Lone Star State: the Wineburgh Philatelic Research Library at the University of Texas at Dallas and the Schmidt Texas Postal History Collection at the University of Texas at Arlington. It is appropriate, therefore, that publication of *Texas on Stamps* this year plays a role in the centennial observance of the Texas Philatelic Association.

Topical collecting is highly flexible and requires a great deal of original research. But therein lies part of its pleasure. Much Texas history and many Texans have been depicted on stamps issued not only by the United States but by various other nations.

This book is divided into three sections: history and events; Texans; and Lone Star locales. The principal criterion for inclusion, of course, has been that each event, person or locale must have been depicted on or can be illustrated by one or more United States or foreign stamps. Not every reader is likely to concur with the author's judgment or advice received from others in every instance.

While *Texas on Stamps* will serve as a useful handbook for collectors, it will also be of interest to readers with an interest in Texas and Texans. As such, it is an addition to literature about the Lone Star State but illustrated in a unique fashion.

Stamps have long been considered an outstanding educational medium and have, in fact, been used as teaching aids in history, geography and various branches of science.

It is my hope that this volume will expand some readers' knowledge of Texas while providing sheer and unexpected enjoyment for others.

Jon L. Allen
Dallas, Texas
October 1995

ACKNOWLEDGMENTS

Since *Texas on Stamps* is my third non-fiction book, all of which have required considerable research, I've learned to appreciate the assistance and support of others. None of these volumes would have been possible without contributors who responded cheerfully to my queries. I acknowledge, therefore, their input, as well as that of those who sent me information anonymously. I'm sure they know who they are. So, here goes! Many thanks to:

Mary Lou Gallegos of the El Paso Convention & Visitors Bureau, Julie Mead and Dana Stephens of the Corpus Christi Convention & Visitors Bureau, Ray Buesing of the World Kite Museum and Hall of Fame, Stern Feinberg of the International Kite Museum, Jean Gilbert of Texas' Office of Comptroller of Public Accounts.

Also, Barry Gore and Flo Oxley of the National Wildflower Research Center, Daniel C. Ruacho of the American Heart Association, Nancy G. Robertson and Carolyn L. Huntoon of the National Aeronautics and Space Administration, Robert O'Connor of the Hertzberg Circus Museum, Louis Jacobs of the Shuler Museum of Paleontology at Southern Methodist University, Christi Witten of the American Quarter Horse Foundation, David Bush of the Galveston Historical Foundation, Timothy R. Spisak of the U.S. Bureau of Mines, Stephanie Stewart of the Dumas Chamber of Commerce, Brett Cohen of the Meadows School of the Arts at SMU.

And, Ruth Ann Rugg of the Amon Carter Museum, Raquel Turrubiates of the Mission Chamber of Commerce, Marla Chaloupka of Mothers Against Drunk Driving, Carolyn Cummings of the Boy Scouts of America, Fred Graham of the Texas Sports Hall of Fame, Lewis B. Smith of the American Cotton Museum, Inc., Mike Moran of the United States Olympic Committee, Bill Carle of the Society for American Baseball Research, Duery Menzies of the Mohair Council of America, Gerald D. Saxon of the Special Collections at the Libraries of the University of Texas at Arlington, David E. Alsobrook of the George H. W. Bush Presidential Library at Texas A&M University, Clydie J. Morgan of American Ex-Prisoners of War, Inc., Larry D. Sall of the Wineburgh Philatelic Research Library at the University of Texas at Dallas, Susan Dixon of the American Philatelic Society, Mary G. Ramos, editor of the *Texas Almanac* and Marie R. Fleming of the Nederland Chamber of Commerce.

I've also received much encouragement and assistance from fellow members of the American Philatelic Society, the American Topical Association and the Texas Philatelic Association. Special thanks are due Joan R. Bleakley, Jane King Fohn, James C. Taylor and Richard L. Thomas. Others include Harlan F. Stone, William A. Coffey, John Tierney, Albert E. Spencer, George Griffenhagen and Fred Foldvary.

Lastly, illustrating the book would not have been possible without the support of several stamp dealers, in particular Charles P. Schwartz, whose sources seem virtually limitless. Others in this category are Fred Schindler, Paul Carlin, Howard DeVoe, Ken Nieser, Frank P. Geiger, Richard Pyznar, Rosemary Rick, Nathan Birman, Jon Denney, James O. Vadeboncoeur, Theodore Champion, Lee Straayer, Joseph Malamud and, last but not least, Maeann Bush, who kept her promise, persevered and found the last few illustrations others had been unable to locate. My deepest thanks to each and every one of them.

I

HISTORY AND EVENTS

1528

Although Alonso Alvarez de Piñeda was the first Spaniard to set foot in Texas while mapping the Gulf Coast in 1519, it was nine years before another would spend much time there, albeit unwillingly.

In 1528, Alvar Nuñez Cabeza de Vaca, a member of the ill-fated Narvaez expedition, found himself shipwrecked with a handful of other survivors on Galveston Island. He lived among various Amerind tribes for eight years, gradually working his way west and then south until he reached the Pacific coast of Mexico and encountered a party of Spanish soldiers.

Either misled by his Indian captors or deluded during his wanderings, his reports of gold and silver to be found in the fabulous "seven cities of Cibola" served to motivate further Spanish exploration during the following decade, although without success.

The saga of Cabeza de Vaca was the subject of an epic Mexican motion picture, written and directed by Nicolas Echevarria in 1993.

1540

Once he'd been appointed Governor of Florida in 1537, Hernando De Soto determined to explore the interior of North America, landing at Mobile Bay with 570 men and 223 horses in May 1539, after having established his base in Cuba.

For the next three years, his expedition traveled west, then north along the Savannah River, through the Blue Ridge country, then across the Mississippi River near present-day Memphis. He was the first European to explore the interior of present-day Tennessee, Arkansas, Texas and Oklahoma as he traveled west above the Canadian River.

De Soto had no desire to treat Indians he encountered with mercy; he was ruthless and accused by contemporaries of killing natives for sport, including those of the helpless Caddoan Confederation in East Texas.

During his expedition's return to Florida, De Soto caught a fever at the mouth of the Red River, died on May 21, 1542, and was buried in the Mississippi River. His deputy, Luis de Moscoso, assumed command, eventually leading 311 survivors of the expedition back to Mexico the following year.

1541

Rumors of cities rich in gold and silver to the north of present-day Mexico prompted Antonio de Mendoza, Viceroy of New Spain, to mount the largest Spanish expedition ever to explore North America, financed largely from his own purse.

He placed Francisco Vasquez de Coronado in command of more than 1,000 men, accompanied by 1,500 horses and mules, herds of cattle and sheep, a few priests and Indian guides.

Between 1540 and 1542, the Coronado Entrada explored much of present-day Arizona, New Mexico, Texas, Oklahoma and Kansas.

Rather than finding cities rich in gold and silver, they discovered primitive Indian pueblos and encampments, vast prairies, herds of buffalo and several pristine rivers.

The expedition's search for riches ended in failure, but its discoveries of the head of the Gulf of California, the Grand Canyon and Palo Duro Canyon have intrigued historians and geographers for four centuries.

1685

René Robert Cavelier, Sieur de la Salle, began his exploration of North America in Canada, then traveled from the Ohio Valley to the mouth of the Mississippi River, where he claimed its entire basin for France. He named it in honor of his royal patron, King Louis XIV: Louisiana.

Following his return to France in triumph, he sailed again for the New World with 300 colonists to establish a settlement at the mouth of the Mississippi. Due to bad weather and poor navigation, they missed their objective and landed on New Year's Day 1685, on Matagorda Bay at the mouth of the Lavaca River. Soon, he lost all four of his vessels. One was taken by pirates, two were wrecked and the last, the *Joli*, returned to France when its captain lost interest in colonization.

La Salle and his men built a fort on Garcitas Creek, but disease and famine took a heavy toll. In January 1687 he and seventeen men left in an attempt to reach the Mississippi and journey north to French Canada. After a falling-out with them, he was murdered by his own men in March 1687.

1803

With the acquisition of 800,000 square miles of North America from France in 1803, President Thomas Jefferson almost doubled the size of the young United States.

The Louisiana Purchase, stretching from the Mississippi River to the Rocky Mountains, however, overlapped conflicting claims. Spain, in particular, disputed the Texas-Louisiana border, a 360-mile strip of land south of the Red River, as well as all of the present-day Texas Panhandle below the Arkansas River.

That dispute was settled by the Transcontinental Treaty of 1819, which fixed a permanent Texas-Louisiana boundary along the Sabine and Red rivers and from thence north on the 100th meridian to the Arkansas River.

Texas remained, therefore, under Spanish control in exchange for ceding Florida to the United States.

Although only a relatively small area of present-day Texas was included in the Louisiana Purchase, it was the first portion for which a border was clearly established by treaty.

1817

One of the most colorful pirates to sail the Spanish Main, Jean Lafitte (1780-1825), relocated his base from Louisiana to Galveston Island, Texas, in 1817. Although he and his men had helped Andrew Jackson win the Battle of New Orleans at the close of the War of 1812, within a few years, like other privateers and smugglers, Lafitte was no longer welcome in Louisiana.

On Galveston Island, according to legend, his town of Campeachy, dominated by his fortified red mansion, had over 200 buildings and a population of 2,200 by the time it was devasted by a hurricane in the summer of 1818. Lafitte and many of his followers remained on Galveston Island for three more years until persuaded to leave as the result of two visits by the United States Navy brigantine *Enterprise*. Lafitte and his remaining men reportedly operated from an island off the Yucatan coast until his death in 1826.

For well over 100 years, treasure seekers were convinced some of Lafitte's booty was buried on Galveston Island, yet none has been found, despite numerous efforts.

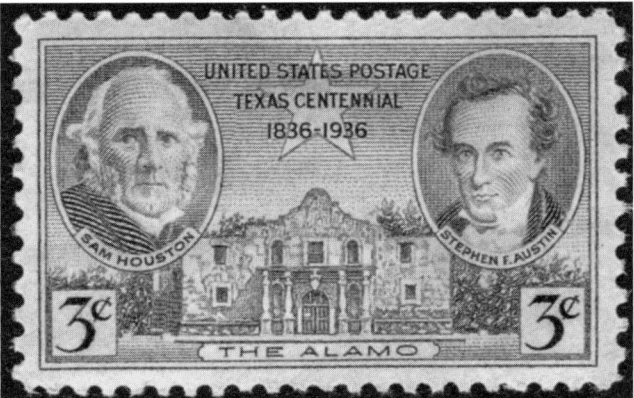

1836

The influx of 20,000 American and European settlers and 4,000 slaves to Texas by 1835, convinced Mexico that the United States had designs on her territory. The following February, General Antonio Lopez de Santa Anna marched into Texas with a large army. As word of his ruthlessness preceded him, thousands of Texans abandoned their homes in panic, their flight becoming known in Texas history as the Runaway Scrape.

Four days prior to the fall of the Alamo on March 6, Texans had convened at Washington-on-the-Brazos where they issued a declaration of independence, drafted a constitution and set up a provisional government.

Santa Anna pursued the remnants of the Texas army east until General Sam Houston elected to make a stand at San Jacinto on April 21. The Texans won a decisive victory, captured Santa Anna and assured the survival of the fledgling republic. A permanent government, with Sam Houston as president, was inaugurated in October 1836.

During its existence for almost a decade, the republic was recognized by the United States, France, Britain and other nations.

1836

No single event in the history of Texas has captured the imagination of Texans, indeed all Americans, as much as the heroic defense of the Alamo in San Antonio.

With only 180 men and eighteen cannons, the defenders under Colonel William B. Travis (1809-1836) held out for thirteen days against an army of 6,000 Mexican regulars led by General Antonio Lopez de Santa Anna, then president of Mexico.

Every defender either perished during the fierce battle or was executed after the Alamo fell to overwhelming odds on March 6. General Santa Anna lost an estimated 1,000 men killed or wounded during the assault.

Besides Colonel Travis, two legendary frontiersmen were killed at the Alamo: David Crockett (1786-1836), a former three-term U.S. congressman from Tennessee, and James Bowie (1796-1836), at the time one of the richest men in Texas with land holdings of 800,000 acres.

1839

The official flag of Texas was adopted by the Third Congress of the Republic on January 25, 1839. It replaced an 1836 design by David G. Burnet which depicted a single gold star on an azure background. The present single white star with five points has given Texas its appelation as the Lone Star State.

The flag's three colors represent the same virtues as the Stars and Stripes: red for courage, white for purity and liberty and blue for loyalty.

The flag was displayed without any rules for its usage for almost one hundred years until guidelines were adopted in 1933. They were codified by the Seventy-third Legislature in 1993.

A total of six flags have flown over Texas in this generally accepted sequence: Spain, 1519-1685; France, 1685-1690; Spain 1690-1821; Mexico, 1821-1836; Republic of Texas, 1836-1845; United States, 1845-1861; Confederate States of America, 1861-1865; and United States, 1865 to the present.

1845

When Texas was formally admitted to the United States as the twenty-eighth state on December 29, 1845, it was a remarkable testament to Sam Houston's political and diplomatic skills and unwavering dedication to annexation.

His representatives in London, Paris, Mexico City and Washington were deliberately unclear about the future of the young republic. Various possibilities were hinted at until Houston and his fellow Texans secured exactly what they wanted. The U.S. Congress passed a joint resolution to annex Texas as a state, not a territory, on February 28, 1845.

When the Texas Congress met on June 16, it voted in favor of annexation and a constitutional convention was convened on July 4 to write a constitution that was ratified in October.

The republic yielded its authority to the United States on February 16, 1846. When the Lone Star flag was lowered three days later, it was presented to Houston, who, along with Thomas Jefferson Rusk, went to Washington as the new state's first U.S. senators.

1846

Mexico adamantly refused to recognize the Republic of Texas throughout its existence and considered the prospect of its annexation by the United States in 1845 a hostile act. Annexation on December 29 led to clashes along the Rio Grande early the following year.

General Zachary Taylor (1784-1850) was encamped with 2,300 men under his command at Corpus Christi when Mexican forces crossed the Rio Grande to attack his outpost at Fort Brown, site of present-day Brownsville, on April 24.

With Texans scouting ahead, General Taylor drove south, relieving Fort Brown on May 7. A succession of victories followed, first at Palo Alto; Matamoros was occupied ten days later. Finally, a resounding defeat for Mexican forces at Buena Vista several months later left northern Mexico in American hands and was credited with helping elect Taylor as twelfth president of the United States two years later.

By the Treaty of Guadalupe Hidalgo of 1848, Mexico agreed to relinquish all claims to Texas and ceded most of Arizona and New Mexico and all of California and Nevada to the United States for a payment of $15 million.

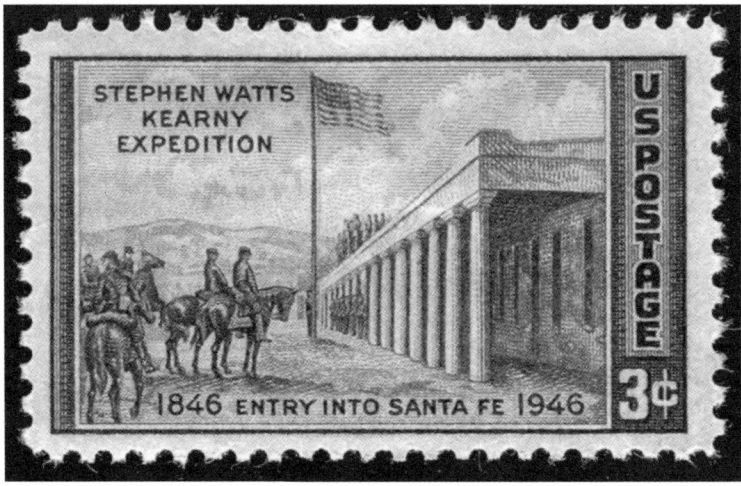

1850

For a decade following independence, Texas claimed more than 360,000 square miles of territory, including half of present-day New Mexico. The claim was based on the contention its border stretched from the mouth of the Rio Grande to its source in the San Juan Mountains of western Colorado. Texas even established a short-lived Santa Fe County.

In 1841 two ill-fated expeditions numbering some 400 men attemped to reach Santa Fe and claim it for Texas. They were intercepted by Mexican militia, captured and force-marched under brutal conditions for 2,000 miles and imprisoned in Mexico City. Many were executed on the trail; others did not survive imprisonment.

During the Mexican War, Colonel Stephen Watts Kearny captured Santa Fe without loss on August 18, 1846. New Mexico would become part of the United States. Although Texas persisted in its claim, its emissaries were rebuffed.

The western and northern boundaries of Texas were fixed permanently by the Compromise of 1850 with a payment of $10 million in compensation for "lost" territory.

1853

The coming of the railroad to Texas was a boon for the state. Between the 1853 establishment of the first line, the Buffalo Bayou, Brazos and Colorado Railroad, and 1904, some 270 companies were formed.

Athough Texas had less than 500 miles of track when the state seceded to join the Confederacy in 1861, construction boomed in the 1870s and 1880s with 8,000 miles of new track connecting the Gulf Coast, South Texas, West Texas and the Panhandle with the rest of the United States. By 1904, the state boasted 10,000 miles of railroad track, more than any other state.

The railroads were able to slash the cost of shipping cotton by two-thirds, and cities such as Fort Worth and Amarillo grew rapidly as rail terminals at the end of great cattle drives.

The role of railroads in the settlement of Texas and the growth of its economy is reflected in the state's ten museums which feature restored depots, locomotives, cars and memorabilia. There are also several short working lines on which visitors can relive the age of steam engines.

1858

From September 1858 to March 1861, the Butterfield Overland Mail linked Missouri and southern California with regular stagecoach service twice weekly in each direction. Of the 3,134 miles covered, 732 were across Texas, from Colbert's Ferry on the Red River near Denison to El Paso. Today, the history of the short-lived service is kept alive in the Overland Trail Museum in Fort Stockton, Texas.

The Butterfield Overland Mail, which also carried passengers, was a mammoth enterprise. Once John Butterfield, a founder of the American Express Company, had secured a mail contract, partly through his personal friendship with President James Buchanan, he had to purchase 250 coaches, freight and tank wagons, more than 6,000 horses and mules, and hire some 2,000 drivers, helpers, mechanics and station managers to staff the route's 200 stations.

The demise of the Butterfield Overland Mail in 1861 was laid to three reasons: tension between northern and southern states, extension of the telegraph and railroad across the continent and, to some extent, brief competition from the Pony Express which operated directly to Sacramento and San Francisco via a northern route.

1875

When their chief Quanah Parker led the last band of Comanche Indians on to a reservation in Oklahoma in June, 1875, it marked the end of 170 years of the tribe's dominance of the Southern Plains. Their horsemanship and fighting spirit were equaled by no other North American tribe.

As Texas' population mushroomed from 35,000 to more than 600,000 in the twenty-five years after independence, the Comanches' nomadic way of life was increasingly imperiled. There were fewer campsites, fewer buffalo to hunt, diminished grazing and more and better-armed adversaries to battle. Their struggle made them the last tribe to accept life on a reservation.

In 1872, Comanches, Cheyennes, Kiowas and Apaches joined together in a final attempt to halt further encroachment on their lands.

Two years later, 1874 effectively marked the end of the Comanche Nation, when Colonel Ranald Mackenzie led 600 troopers into Palo Duro Canyon on the morning of September 28, surprising their last large war party in their teepees.

1890

Texas was truly the nation's Cattle Kingdom throughout the second half of the nineteenth century. Between the end of the Civil War in 1865 and 1890, hundreds of great trail drives delivered more than ten million Longhorn cattle to railheads at Wichita, Abilene and Dodge City.

Open range soon gave way, however, to vast ranches, such as the King, XIT, JA and Matador, enclosed by several hundred miles of barbed wire and irrigated by as many as 300 windmills.

With the arrival of the railroad, great trail drives were no longer necessary. A new breed soon supplanted the hardy Longhorn. The first such native to America and the first new breed in 200 years, the Santa Gertrudis, a combination of Shorthorns and Brahmans, proved able to cope with Texas' heat, insects and disease while yielding several hundred more pounds of beef than the Longhorn.

Today, raising beef cattle remains the state's dominant agricultural industry with some 13,600,000 head in the state, or fourteen percent of all beef cattle in the U.S. Sales are conducted annually at 145 regulated livestock auctions.

1898

Within a month after the United States declared war on Spain in April 1898, Theodore Roosevelt (1858-1919) resigned his post as assistant secretary of the Navy to form the 1st Volunteer U.S. Cavalry Regiment. His 1,000 "Rough Riders," composed of ranchers, former Texas Rangers and cowhands from the Southwest, assembled in San Antonio to train for the invasion of Cuba.

Dubbed "the cowboy cavalry," they were an unorthodox formation but distinguished themselves in assaults on Kettle Hill and San Juan Hill after their arrival in Cuba. The unit's original commander, Colonel Leonard Wood, upon being promoted to brigadier general, turned over his command to Roosevelt. Historians agree the latter's leadership of the "Rough Riders" propelled him into the governorship of New York in 1899 and the vice presidency of the United States in 1900. When President William McKinley died at the hands of an assassin on September 14, 1901, Roosevelt became the twenty-fifth president of the United States and was re-elected in 1904. He was awarded the Nobel Peace Prize in 1906.

1900

Cotton production in Texas began around the Spanish missions in the 1740s and by the end of the nineteenth century had become a major source of wealth. According to historical records, the state produced 3,438,000 bales on seven thousand acres in 1900.

Since 1880, Texas had led the nation in production, shipping a third of the crop produced in the United States. Much of the state's billion dollar annual production is exported, principally to Asia, with less than ten percent processed within Texas.

Greenville, site of the world's record for a single day's bale production of 2,073 bales in 1912, is also the location of the American Cotton Museum. Its current facility is being expanded to a five-building complex scheduled for completion after 1998. A noteworthy feature in the museum is the world's largest inland cotton compress which stands three and one-half stories high.

1901

In addition to its flag and official seal, a state customarily adopts various additional symbols, usually native flora and fauna.

In Texas, the first such was the bluebonnet (*Lupinus Texensis*), selected as the official state flower in 1901 by the Twenty-seventh Texas Legislature.

Then, in 1927, at the request of the Texas Federation of Women's Clubs, the mockingbird (*Mimus polyglottos*) was chosen as official state bird by the Fortieth Legislature.

It didn't stop there.

The lightning whelk was adopted as Texas' official state seashell by the Seventieth Legislature in 1987. It's named for its colored stripes and is found only on the Gulf Coast.

Not to be outdone, Texas' Seventy-fourth Legislature designated official small and large mammals in 1995, the former being the armadillo and the latter the Longhorn.

There is also an official state gem, tree, insect, fruit, grass, fish and others duly approved by the Texas Legislature.

1901

In 1899, the United States Geological Survey released a report which, fortunately, had no effect whatsoever on the future of Texas. It concluded there was "little or no chance" oil would ever be discovered in Texas.

Less than two years later on January 10, 1901, the largest oil field in the world at the time blew its first gusher 200 feet into the air at Spindletop near Beaumont.

Further discoveries followed—in East Texas, West Texas, the Panhandle and, later, offshore in the Gulf of Mexico.

Texas soon became synonymous with oil, and Texas-based companies took the lead in worldwide exploration.

King Cotton and the Cattle Kingdom had brought wealth to the Lone Star State in the nineteenth century. For the next one hundred years, petroleum production and refining would far outstrip their role in the state's economy. Oil would become a truly international business with Texans at the forefront on every continent.

1910

San Antonio has long been considered the birthplace of the U.S. Air Force. Of the four bases there, Randolph Air Force Base was known informally as the "West Point of the Air."

In February 1910, American airpower consisted of one frail, damaged aircraft, constructed by Wilbur and Orville Wright, and one unqualified officer, Lieutenant Benjamin D. Foulois (1879-1967), who'd been sent to Fort Sam Houston in San Antonio to teach himself to fly. As he had no instructor, every flight was solo, but he corresponded with the Wright brothers for guidance.

By 1916, his First Aero Squadron had eight planes and flew in support of General John J. Pershing's foray into Mexico. When Pershing became commander of the American Expeditionary Force in France in World War I, Foulois assumed command of the Air Service as a brigadier general.

After serving as chief of the Air Corps from 1931 to 1935, Foulois retired as a major general, but lived well past World War II, during which American industry produced almost 300,000 military aircraft for the United States and its Allies.

1916

After crossing the border from Mexico in 1912, the Mexican revolutionary Francisco "Pancho" Villa (1878-1923) reorganized his followers in El Paso, Texas, where he resided at 609 North Oregon Street. They returned to the State of Chihuahua the following year.

He made two serious blunders in 1916, first when he massacred fifteen Americans at Santa Isabel, then, again two months later when he crossed the border into Lincoln, New Mexico, this time killing another seventeen on American soil.

General John J. Pershing (1860-1948) led a swift, long-range expedition against Villa later that year. Villa's forces were effectively disbanded, although he was never captured.

Pershing later commanded the American Expeditionary Force in France after the U.S. entered World War I, while one of his young staff officers, Captain George S. Patton (1885-1945), would become one of the outstanding military leaders of World War II.

1927

For fifteen of his seventy years, sculptor Gutzon Borglum (1871-1941) made his home in San Antonio, a city he called his adopted home. While he maintained an apartment at the Menger Hotel, he built five-foot models for his major achievement, Mount Rushmore, in his Brackenridge Park studio.

Prior to moving to Texas in 1927, he'd already completed a memorial to the Confederate States of America at Stone Mountain, Georgia. While he was in Texas, he executed many commissions for works in North Carolina, Arizona, New York, the District of Columbia and Europe.

One major work for which he was engaged in Texas was the Trail Drivers Memorial at the Witte Museum in San Antonio. However, despite his international reputation, he was frustrated by lack of recognition in Texas, terming works by others commissioned for the centennial of Texas' statehood in 1936, "frightful, aesthetic failures."

After his death on March 6, 1941, his son, Lincoln Borglum, completed Mount Rushmore, then stayed in Beeville and Harlingen with his Texas-born wife, Louella Jones Borglum.

1942

Once legislation enabling women to serve in uniform had been signed into law in 1942, Army Chief of Staff General George C. Marshall personally selected a director for the Women's Army Corps. His choice was Oveta Culp Hobby, born in Killeen, Texas, on January 19, 1905. Mrs. Hobby, the wife of former Governor William P. Hobby, was already a successful newspaper editor and publisher in her own right.

During the war, more than 100,000 women served in the Corps. Many were assigned menial duties, except in the Army Air Forces where every non-combat assignment and school was open to them. Almost 10,000 WACs served in Europe and North Africa, including a select group, fluent in French, assigned to General Dwight D. Eisenhower's headquarters. General Douglas MacArthur called the 6,000 WACs who served under him in the South Pacific "some of my best soldiers."

After the war, Mrs. Hobby returned to Houston as a newspaper and television executive, with time out from 1953 to 1955 to serve as secretary of Health, Education and Welfare in the Eisenhower administration. She died in Houston, Texas, on August 16, 1995.

1963

Rivers tend to meander or change direction because their flow isn't always predictable. The Rio Grande, which defines much of the 2,000-mile border between the United States and Mexico, is no exception.

For almost a century, the United States and Mexico disputed where the banks of the Rio Grande should be at El Paso/Juárez. Then, in 1963, Presidents John F. Kennedy and Adolfo López Mateos signed the Chamizal Treaty, implemented five years later by Presidents Lyndon B. Johnson and Gustavo Díaz Ordas.

The treaty ceded land beside the river to Mexico, but the two nations agreed to establish parks on both sides of the border.

Today, the Chamizal National Memorial on the United States side of the border is an elegant fifty-five-acre public park boasting a museum, annual festivals and dramas which highlight the United States-Mexico border cultural heritage. These are sponsored by the U.S. National Park Service.

1963

Just after midday on November 22, 1963, John F. Kennedy, thirty-fifth president of the United States, became the nation's fourth president to die at the hands of an assassin. He was struck by two bullets in his neck and head during a motorcade shortly after his arrival in Dallas for a speech. He was pronounced dead at that city's Parkland Memorial Hospital less than half an hour later.

Vice President Lyndon B. Johnson of Texas was sworn in as his successor aboard the presidential aircraft, Air Force One, at Dallas' Love Field two hours later.

A permanent exhibit on the life, death and legacy of President Kennedy is located on the sixth floor of the former Texas School Book Depository Building from which the shots were fired. Nearby, a cenotaph and memorial park also honor the slain president.

1968

San Antonio played host to millions of visitors from April to October 1968 as site of the first world's fair to be held in Texas. It was also a celebration of the 250th anniversary of the city's founding by Martín de Alarcón as Villa de Bexar on April 25, 1718.

Twenty-five foreign nations and numerous industrial and cultural organizations erected pavilions on the ninety-two-acre grounds of HemisFair '68 which were dominated by a 622-foot spire, the Tower of the Americas, featuring restaurants, gift shops and two observation decks.

The grounds of the fair were planned as a permanent civic center close to the Alamo, La Villita and the city's popular river walk, connected to HemisFair '68 by a lagoon and canal. Among the legacies of the fair are a convention center, a museum of Texas history, a federal courthouse and office complex, several well-preserved historic buildings relocated from other parts of the city, and murals and sculptures by noted artists from several nations.

1994

When the Fifteenth World Cup soccer championship was held in the United States in 1994, it was the first time the United States had hosted this international event.

Dallas was one of nine cities selected to host playoff games. Moreover, Dallas was chosen as the site of the international broadcast center from which television and radio coverage was beamed by satellite to 120 nations with an estimated audience of over one billion viewers and listeners.

Twenty-four nations qualified to compete in the 1994 World Cup Championships. Half of them played six matches to sell-out crowds at the Cotton Bowl in Dallas.

Final victory in Los Angeles on July 17 went to Brazil, which defeated Italy in a penalty kick shootout to win its fouth World Cup title.

The 1994 World Cup was the most watched television event in history. It was also the best-attended World Cup ever with 3,567,994 spectators attending the fifty-two matches.

TEXANS

GENE AUTRY

The son of a Baptist minister, Orvon "Gene" Autry was born in Tioga Springs on September 29, 1907. He was encouraged in his career by Will Rogers and went on to become the most successful singing cowboy of all time. He appeared in over 100 motion pictures and his horse, Champion, became a celebrity in his own right.

Among Autry's greatest single hits were "Mexicali Rose," "Tumbling Tumbleweeds," "Frosty The Snowman, "Here Comes Peter Cottontail" and his longtime theme song, "Back in the Saddle Again." He and his comic sidekicks, Smiley Burnette and Pat Buttram, were popular with kids worldwide.

During World War II, Autry interrupted his career to fly in Burma, enabling Roy Rogers to take his place in musical westerns.

A successful businessman, Autry has owned a television production company, hotels, radio stations and the Los Angeles Angels baseball team. He was elected to the Country Music Hall of Fame in 1969.

ERNIE BANKS

During his career with the Chicago Cubs, Ernie Banks played 2,528 games between 1953 and 1971, hitting 1,574 singles, 407 doubles, ninety triples and 512 home runs.

Born in Dallas on January 31, 1931, the eleven-time all-star was inducted into the Baseball Hall of Fame in 1977 and similarly honored by the Texas Sports Hall of Fame.

He led the National League in home runs in 1958 with forty-seven, then again in 1960 with forty-one. He was named the league's most valuable player in both 1958 and 1959. His batting average in 1959 was .304. At shortstop, Banks led the league in fielding percentage three times in eight seasons.

In 1970, he played part-time, and in 1971 appeared in only thirty-nine games. He announced his retirement in 1971.

Known for his ready smile and cheerful attitude, Banks was nicknamed "Mr. Cub" and voted the team's best player ever by Cubs fans in 1969.

ALAN L. BEAN

Navy Captain Alan L. Bean walked on the moon as pilot of Apollo XII, man's second moon landing, in November 1969, then went on to command Skylab II, a fifty-nine-day record mission from July to September 1973. The following year, Captain Bean served as backup spacecraft commander for the joint United States-Russian Apollo-Soyuz Test Project.

He was born in Wheeler, Texas, on March 15, 1932, and graduated from Paschal High School in Fort Worth in 1951. He was awarded a degree in aeronautical engineering from the University of Texas in 1955. Commissioned as a naval officer in 1955, he won his wings the following year and served as a fighter pilot and test pilot until selected for astronaut training by NASA in October 1963.

Captain Bean retired from the United States Navy in October 1975 and from NASA in June 1981. During his career, he flew twenty-seven types of military aircraft. He has since worked as an artist to capture on canvas the visions he observed in space.

George H.W. Bush, U.S. President

GEORGE H. W. BUSH

In November 1988, George H. W. Bush of Houston was elected forty-first president of the United States, following eight years as vice president in the two administrations of President Ronald Reagan.

The son of a U.S. Senator, Bush served as a naval aviator in World War II. After graduation from Yale University in 1948, he moved to Texas to enter the oil industry. He was elected to the U.S. House of Representatives in the Texas Seventh Congressional District in 1966, serving two terms.

Defeated in a race for the U.S. Senate in 1970, he spent the next decade serving in high government and political posts, including U.S. Ambassador to the United Nations, Chairman of the Republican National Committee, Special Envoy to the People's Republic of China and Director of the Central Intelligence Agency.

Despite early victories in the primaries, he lost the Republican nomination for president in 1980 to Ronald Reagan, joining the ticket as nominee for vice president.

The campus of Texas A&M University in College Station has been selected as the site of his presidential library.

CLAIRE LEE CHENNAULT

Born in Commerce on September 6, 1890, Claire L. Chennault was a military aviator forced to retire from the U.S. Army Air Corps as a lieutenant colonel because of a hearing disability in 1937. Later that year, he organized the American Volunteer Group (AVG) to help China resist Japanese aggression. His outfit, dubbed "The Flying Tigers," downed 299 Japanese aircraft in six months with the loss of only ten American pilots.

In April 1942, Chennault was recalled to active duty in the U.S. Army Air Forces and promoted to the grade of major general the following March, in command of the U.S. Fourteenth Air Force. A brilliant tactician and aggressive commander, Chennault is the author of one book, *The Role of Defensive Pursuit*, and several articles on fighter tactics.

He retired from the U.S. Army Air Forces in October 1945, then returned to China to establish a commercial airline (CAT). He came back to the United States for medical treatment in 1958 and died in New Orleans on July 27, 1958.

BESSIE COLEMAN

Born in Atlanta on January 26, 1892, and raised in Waxahachie, Bessie Coleman set her sights on the sky at an early age. Her determination to become the first African-American woman to earn a pilot's license took her to France, after she was rejected in her own country. After seven months of instruction, she earned her international pilot's license on June 15, 1921.

Returning to America, "Queen Bess," as she became known, barnstormed, performing stunts and aerobatics, spoke to school and church audiences and promoted aviation as a career for African-Americans.

Her major unfulfilled ambition was to found a flying school in the Chicago area to pass her love of aviation on to others. She died on April 30, 1926, at the age of thirty-four as a passenger in a plane piloted by her mechanic; the plane's controls jammed, causing the crash.

Bessie Coleman's original pilot's license and other memorabilia are displayed at the DuSable Museum of African American History in Chicago.

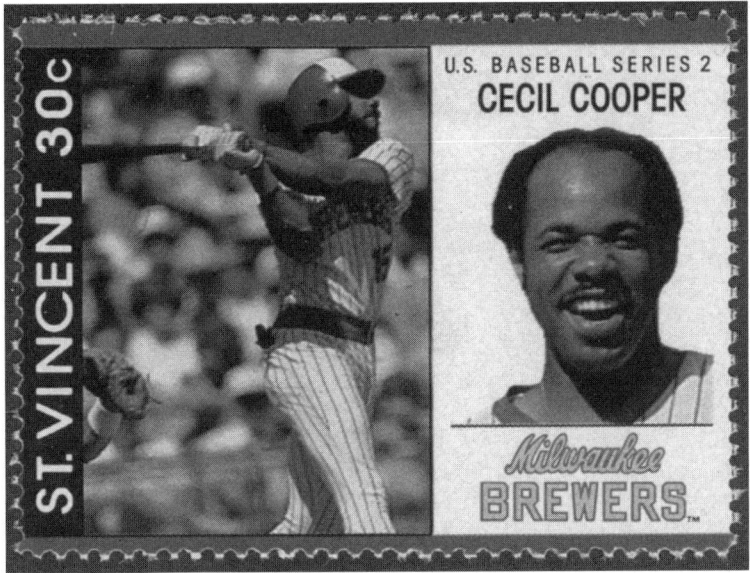

CECIL COOPER

After playing for two state high school championship baseball teams and attending Prairie View A&M College, Cecil Cooper was drafted by the Boston Red Sox in June 1968.

He was born in Brenham on December 20, 1949, the youngest of thirteen children; two of his older brothers also played baseball.

After the minor leagues, Cooper became a regular Red Sox first baseman in 1974 but was traded to the Milwaukee Brewers in 1976. He quickly became a star performer, batting over .300 for six consecutive seasons and winning the Gold Glove Award twice.

A four-time all-star, he played in the 1975 World Series with the Red Sox and in the 1982 Series with the Brewers, setting a record in the latter with ten assists by a first baseman. His career batting average through 1986 was .300, with 2,130 hits, 402 doubles and 235 home runs. He won the 1983 Roberto Clemente Award for humanitarian work with Athletes for Youth in Milwaukee.

ROBERT L. CRIPPEN

Robert L. Crippen piloted four space shuttle flights: *Columbia* in April 1981; *Challenger* in June 1983; Challenger again in April 1984 and October 1984.

He was born in Beaumont on September 11, 1937. After graduation from high school in Caney, he was awarded a degree in aerospace engineering at the University of Texas in 1960.

Crippen was commissioned as a naval aviator in 1962, serving as an attack pilot until chosen to attend the U.S. Air Force Aerospace Research Pilot School at Edwards AFB, California. He was selected for astronaut training by NASA in September 1969.

Subsequent to his retirement from the U.S. Navy in the grade of captain with 6,500 hours flying time, he continued to serve NASA as director of the Kennedy Space Center. Among his numerous awards and decorations the Harmon Trophy (1982), the Goddard Trophy (1982) and the National Geographic Society's Hubbard Medal (1981) are especially significant.

DWIGHT D. EISENHOWER

Born in Denison on October 14, 1890, Dwight D. Eisenhower was raised in Kansas until, in 1911, he won an appointment to the United States Military Academy. After his graduation with the Class of 1915, he and fifty-eight of his 163 classmates would later become generals.

After a series of staff assignments during twenty peacetime years, he rose rapidly in rank when the United States entered World War II, commanding the Allied invasion of North Africa, then the Normandy landings as supreme commander with the rank of five-star general.

He retired in 1948 to assume the presidency of Columbia University but returned to active duty two years later as supreme commander of NATO.

In 1952, he retired again to accept the Republican nomination for the presidency of the United States. He was elected and served two terms, from 1953 to 1961, as the thirty-fourth president of the United States.

He died in Washington, D.C., on March 28, 1969.

GEORGE FOREMAN

After only eighteen amateur fights as a heavyweight boxer, George Foreman made the U.S. Olympic team in 1968, won the gold medal in Mexico City and achieved lasting fame for carrying a small American flag around the ring. He was born in Marshall on January 22, 1948.

He turned professional the year after his triumph at the Olympic Games, winning all thirty-four of his fights. Then, on January 22, 1973, he defeated Joe Frazier in less than two rounds to win the heavyweight championship.

After losing his title to Muhammad Ali in 1974, he won five more fights before retiring in 1977. He fought again from 1977 to 1987, coming out of his second retirement in 1993 to challenge Michael Moorer for the heavyweight title. He won by a knockout in the tenth round, becoming at the age of forty-six the oldest champion ever in any weight division. He won seventy-three of his seventy-seven professional fights.

An extremely popular personality, Foreman is highly regarded for his sense of humor and charitable work.

ANTHONY JOSEPH FOYT

The only driver to win the Indianapolis 500 four times, A.J. Foyt is also the only race car driver to win the Daytona 500 and the Twenty-four Hours at LeMans as well.

Foyt was born in Houston on January 16, 1935, and started racing professionally at the age of eighteen, qualifying for his first Indianapolis 500 at the age of twenty-three. He won in 1961, 1964, 1967 and 1977. He also won forty-eight races in stock cars, twenty-nine in sprint cars, twenty-one in midget cars, seven in sports cars and two in championship dirt track cars.

He is the only driver to win races on oval speedways, road courses and dirt tracks in a single season — in 1968.

An astute businessman, Foyt owns the largest automobile dealership in Texas, has interests in oil wells, a hotel chain and the largest funeral service company in the nation.

He is a member of the Indianapolis Speedway Hall of Fame and of the Texas Sports Hall of Fame. He was still racing competitively in 1995 at age sixty.

CHARLES C. GOODNIGHT

During the decade of the great cattle drives with herds of more than a thousand cattle on the trail, one name stands out above all others, that of Charles C. Goodnight (1836-1929), who lent his name to the Goodnight and Goodnight-Loving trails.

Goodnight had served as a ranger during the 1850s when marauding Indians and Mexican bandits attacked settlers and travelers alike. By the end of the Civil War in 1865, Colonel Goodnight was highly regarded throughout Texas.

After he married Mary Ann Dyer of Weatherford in 1870 he resolved to settle down as a cattle rancher. In 1876, with financial backing from a partner, John Adair, he established the JA Ranch in Palo Duro Canyon with 1,600 head of cattle he had trailed down from Colorado to escape the approaching winter. It was the first ranch in the Texas Panhandle.

Much of the JA Ranch is today part of the 15,100-acre Palo Duro Canyon State Park, one of the largest in the state. When the National Cowboy Hall of Fame was founded in Oklahoma City in 1965, Charles C. Goodnight was its first honoree.

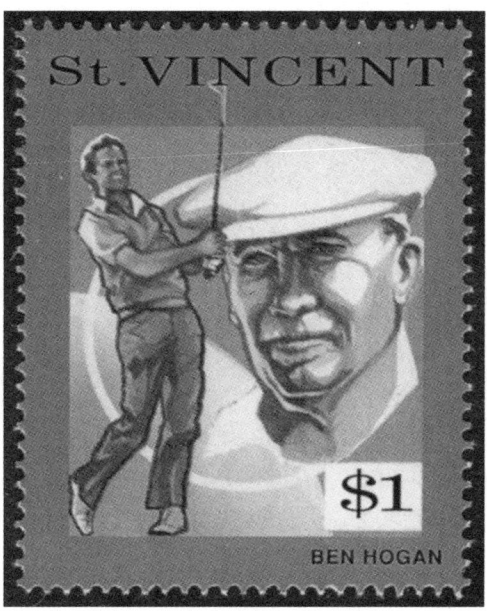

BEN HOGAN

One of the greatest golfers of his generation, William Benjamin Hogan won five tournaments in 1941 and became the top money winner on the Professional Golf Association Tour in 1940, 1941 and 1942 before serving in the Army Air Corps during World War II. He was born in Dublin on August 13, 1912.

After rejoining the PGA tour in 1945, he won thirty-five titles prior to a devastating automobile accident in February 1949 in which he saved the life of his wife, Valerie, by throwing his body in front of her just before impact. Hogan worked hard on rehabilitation and was playing golf again in less than a year.

Prior to his retirement from competition in 1960, Hogan had posted four victories in the U.S. Open, two at the PGA, two at the Masters in Augusta, Georgia, and one at the 1953 British Open, which he won the first and only time he entered.

Hogan was admired by American and British galleries alike for his icy, detached style from tee to green.

BUDDY HOLLY

A musician whose country melody was tinged with a blues inflection and pioneering rock n' roll technique, Charles Hardin "Buddy" Holly gave the world recordings that never seem to lose their freshness.

He was born in Lubbock on September 7, 1936, and died on tour at the age of twenty-two in a plane crash with fellow musicians Ritchie Valens and J. P. "Big Bopper" Richardson near Clear Lake, Iowa, on February 3, 1959.

He and his group, the Crickets, were more successful in Britain and Australia than in the U.S. Among their most popular recordings were "Rave On," "That'll Be The Day," "Words of Love," "It Doesn't Matter Any More," "Every Day" and "Peggy Sue." The latter was featured on the soundtrack of the 1986 motion picture *Peggy Sue Got Married.*

Holly is buried in the City of Lubbock Cemetery on East 34th Street and a statue of him with guitar in hand on Avenue Q honors him and other West Texas musicians who have made imporant contributions to the world of popular music.

SAM HOPKINS

Blues music developed gradually throughout the southern United States, with Texas musicians playing a prominent role as the form evolved. One of the most notable was Sam Hopkins, born in Centerville on March 12, 1912, and raised in Leona. During his career, Sam "Lightnin'" Hopkins composed more than 600 songs.

Hopkins was a blues singer, superb guitarist and a consummate minstrel. He picked up his nickname by chance in 1946 while performing with pianist Wilson "Thunder" Smith for Aladdin Records.

During his career, he progressed from playing and singing on city buses in Houston to an appearance at Carnegie Hall in 1960. Thereafter, he recorded his original material for several major labels: Candid, Prestige, Folkways, Heritage, Transition and, with his brother, John Henry Hopkins, the Arhoolie label.

Sam Hopkins died in Houston on January 30, 1982, but his music lives on in his many recordings and motion picture sound tracks.

ROGERS HORNSBY

Records had a way of falling for Rogers Hornsby whose talent at hitting baseballs enabled him to keep on setting new ones. In 2,259 games, his career average of .358 is a National League record and his .424 average in the 1924 season is a major league record in the twentieth century.

Hornsby was born in Winters on April 27, 1896, and joined the St. Louis Cardinals at the end of the 1916 season. Starting in 1920, he won six straight batting titles. In 1925, he won the National League's Most Valuable Player Award and was selected to succeed Branch Rickey as manager. The following year, he led St. Louis to a seven-game World Series victory over the New York Yankees.

Outspoken, he often had problems with management. After leaving St. Louis, he played for the New York Giants, the Boston Braves, Chicago Cubs and St. Louis Browns and coached the Cincinnati Reds and New York Mets. He was elected to the Baseball Hall of Fame and the Texas Sports Hall of Fame. He died on January 5, 1963.

SAMUEL HOUSTON

By the time he arrived in Texas at the age of forty, Sam Houston (1793-1863) had lived with Cherokee Indians for several years, become a lifelong friend of Andrew Jackson and served two terms as a U.S. congressman and one as a popular governor of Tennessee.

On March 2, 1836, he was one of the signers of the Texas Declaration of Independence. He then assumed command of the fledgling republic's army, avenging the massacres of fellow Texans at the Alamo and Goliad with a stunning victory over Santa Anna at the Battle of San Jacinto on April 21.

Subsequently, he served twice as president of the Republic of Texas. Following statehood in 1846, he was a U.S. senator for thirteen years. In 1859, he returned to Texas and was elected governor. Adamantly opposed to secession, he resigned in 1861 rather than swear allegiance to the Confederacy. He died of pneumonia on July 26, 1863, in Huntsville, where a museum, library and visitor center honor his memory. The state's largest city bears his name.

LYNDON BAINES JOHNSON

After a couple of years as a teacher in South Texas, Lyndon B. Johnson accepted an appointment in 1932 to the staff of Congressman Richard M. Kleberg. He never looked back. An ardent supporter of the New Deal, he was elected to the House of Representatives in 1937 and the United States Senate in 1948. By 1953, he was the majority leader in the upper house.

Johnson was born in Stonewall on August 27, 1908. After serving in the U.S. Navy in World War II, he dedicated his life to public service. As vice president of the United States, he succeeded John F. Kennedy as thirty-fifth president of the United States, following the Kennedy's assassination on November 22, 1963. His presidency was noted for civil rights legislation, Medicare and the war on poverty, together known as the Great Society program.

He did not seek re-election in 1968, largely due to the unpopularity of his stand on the Vietnam conflict. He retired to his ranch in Texas and suffered a fatal heart attack on January 22, 1973.

RAFER L. JOHNSON

Born in Hillsboro on August 18, 1935, Rafer Johnson grew up in the small agricultural community of Kingsburg in the San Joaquin Valley of California.

An outstanding basketball, football and baseball player in high school, he was attracted to the decathlon as a teenager because of its all-around challenge. At age twenty, he set a new world record of 7,985 points in 1955.

He went on to win the event at the 1955 Pan American Games, then set a new world record of 8,302 points in 1958. At the 1960 Olympic Games, he was the first African-American athlete selected to carry his country's flag at the opening ceremonies and went on to win the decathlon gold medal with 8,392 points. His victory was especially remarkable since he had suffered a back injury in a 1959 automobile accident.

Johnson was elected to the National Track & Field Hall of Fame and the Olympic Hall of Fame. In 1984, he was selected to light the flame at the Olympic Games in Los Angeles, California.

GEORGE JONES

Highly admired within and outside the world of country music, George Jones recorded more than 250 albums during his stormy career. He was born in Saratoga on September 12, 1931. Following a stint in the U.S. Marine Corps, he signed with the Starday label in 1952, where he remained for sixteen years.

In February 1969, he married vocalist Tammy Wynette. Together, they recorded some of the finest duets in country music until their talents and personalities, ever in conflict, led to the divorce of the king and queen of country music in March 1975.

His singles topped the country music charts throughout the 1950s and 1960s with titles such as "Why Baby Why," "Heartbreak Hotel," "Tender Years," and "White Lightning."

After declaring bankruptcy in 1979, followed by medical treatment for substance abuse, he made a dramatic comeback, recording his first gold album in 1980 and duets with Willie Nelson, Merle Haggard and his former wife, Tammy Wynette.

JANIS JOPLIN

One of the most successful blues singers of the 1960s, Janis Joplin also had an early interest in poetry and painting. Born in Port Arthur on January 19, 1943, she left home as a teenager to sing in clubs in Houston, Austin and San Antonio.

Her greatest success came in the San Francisco Bay Area, recording on the Mainstream and Columbia labels, with Big Brother and The Holding Company. Later, she formed her own group, the Kozmic Blues Band, with Sam Andrew on guitar, and, in 1970, the new Full Tilt Boogie Band.

Always giving her utmost, she masked a vulnerability beneath a spirited and suggestive style as though she sensed her time was limited. On October 4, 1970, she died in Hollywood, California, from an accidental overdose of heroin. Her legacy endures, however. Several of her recordings were released posthumously in the 1970s and 1980s. The 1979 motion picture *The Rose*, featuring Bette Midler, was based loosely on Joplin's life.

It is interesting to note that Janis' name is misspelled on the stamp pictured above.

SCOTT JOPLIN

The indisputable King of Ragtime, Scott Joplin was born in Texarkana on November 24, 1868. During his lifetime, he wrote akout fifty piano rags. One of the first, composed in 1899, was "Maple Leaf Rag," which sold over a million copies, easily the biggest ragtime hit ever.

At the time, it was unusual for a black musician to be paid in royalties, but publisher John Stark's willingness to do so gave Joplin financial independence.

He also wrote for musicals and ballet and composed at least two operas. Use of his music on the soundtrack of the film *The Sting* in 1974 helped revive interest in his work. His only surviving opera, *Treemonisha,* was never performed professionally in his lifetime but had its premier in 1976 to critical acclaim.

Joplin died in a mental hospital in New York on April 11, 1917. He was awarded a posthumous Pulitzer Prize for his work in 1976.

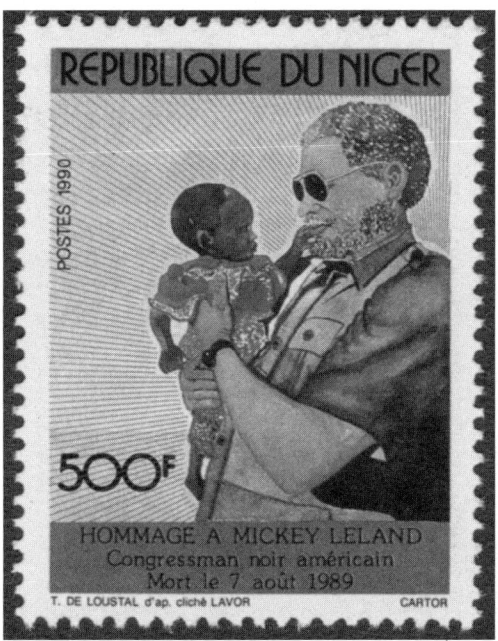

GEORGE THOMAS LELAND

Born in Lubbock on November 27, 1944, George Thomas "Mickey" Leland grew up in Houston and graduated from the Texas Southern University School of Pharmacy in 1970.

First elected to the Texas Legislature in 1972, he served three terms in Austin prior to running for the United States Congress in 1978. He was re-elected in the Eighteenth Congressional District of Texas five times.

Deeply concerned with health and nutrition, he served as chairman of the House Select Committee on Hunger from its inception and was elected chairman of the Congressional Black Caucus in the Ninety-ninth Congress.

During his service in Congress, Leland chaired hearings on hunger and malnutrition and made six trips to Africa to visit refugee camps there. He was killed on August 7, 1989, in the crash of a small aircraft in a remote region of Ethiopia. A federal office builing in Houston is named in his honor and several awards and lectures bear his name.

MANCE LIPSCOMB

A tenant farmer most of his life, Mance Lipscomb played spirituals, ragtime and blues for friends and neighbors for fifty years, leaving his native Texas for the first time at the age of sixty-six. He was born in Navasota on April 9, 1895.

He would have remained an unknown talent had not two collectors of folk music discovered him in 1960. His earthy singing style and ability on the slide guitar made him an outstanding performer in the Texas tradition. Once he'd been recorded, he quickly became one of the best-loved musicians of the country blues genre.

Between 1962 and 1972, he recorded six albums, mostly on the Arhoolie label, and was featured in the motion picture, *A Well Spent Life*. Lipscomb influenced many young rock musicians in the United States and England following his successful appearance at the Folk Musical Festival in Berkeley, California, in 1962.

Mance Lipscomb died on January 30, 1976, at the age of eighty.

GREGORY A. MADDUX

A remarkably consistent baseball pitcher, Greg Maddux won two consecutive National League Cy Young Awards as best pitcher with two different teams in 1992 and 1993. The first with 199 strikeouts was for the Chicago Cubs, while the next was for the Atlanta Braves with 197 strikeouts.

Maddux was born in San Angelo on April 14, 1966. He played his first season in the major leagues in 1986 with the Chicago Cubs. He became a full-time starter in the 1988 season and had a winning record for three out of the next four years. In his two award-winning seasons his record was 20-11 and 20-10.

During his first nine seasons on the mound in the major leagues, he posted a 131-91 record, with seventeen shutouts, striking out 1,190 batters.

In September 1986, he pitched against the Philadelphia Phillies and his brother, Mike Maddux, winning the game. It was the first time brothers had pitched for opposing teams during their rookie years.

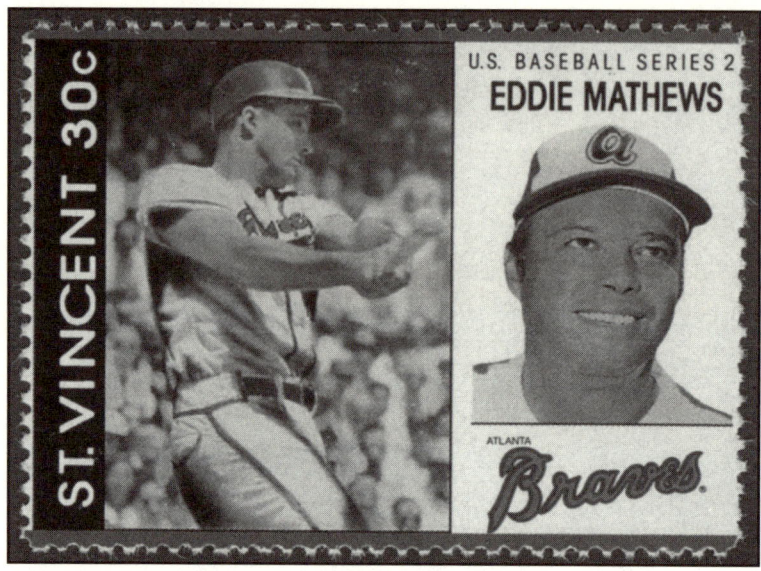

EDWIN L. MATHEWS

An outstanding third baseman with a strong arm, Eddie Mathews was also a dangerous hitter. He was the only player to play for the Braves in Boston, Milwaukee and Atlanta. He played one season each for the Houston Astros and Detroit Tigers in 1967 and 1968, prior to retiring.

Mathews was born in Texarkana on October 13, 1931. He signed with Boston the same day he graduated from high school.

He led the National League in home runs in 1953 with forty-seven and again in 1959 with forty-six. In the next six seasons he hit at least twenty-three in each, and three times hit over thirty.

Mathews and Henry Aaron formed a powerful 1-2 batting combination. He scored four runs and batted in four more in Milwaukee's 1957 World Series victory over the New York Yankees.

In 2,391 games, Mathews hit 512 home runs, 354 doubles and seventy-two triples. He scored a total of 1,509 runs.

He was elected to the Baseball Hall of Fame in 1978.

RANDY MATSON

As a student at Texas A&M University, Randy Matson was the NCAA champion in both discus and shot put events in 1966 and 1967. He had already broken the world record for the shot put in 1965 with a throw af 70,' 7.25", then went on to exceed his own record in 1967 with a throw of 71,' 5.50".

Matson was born in Kilgore on March 5, 1945, and was outstanding in high school basketball and football.

National shot put champion in 1964 and again from 1966 to 1971, he won gold medals in the event at the 1967 Pan American Games and 1968 Olympic Games.

In 1967, he was the recipient of the Sullivan Award as the nation's outstanding amateur athlete. Subsequently he was elected to the National Track & Field Hall of Fame and the Texas Sports Hall of Fame.

After graduating from Texas A&M, he was drafted by National Football League and National Basketball Association teams but chose to retire from competition in 1972.

EDGAR D. MITCHELL

Born on September 17, 1930, in Hereford, Edgar D. Mitchell attended schools in Roswell and Artesia, New Mexico. He graduated from Carnegie-Mellon University in 1952 and later received a Ph.D. in aeronautics and astronautics from the Massachusetts Institute of Technology.

Commissioned as a naval officer in May 1953, he completed pilot training the following year, subsequently serving aboard two aircraft carriers. From 1959 to 1965, he was assigned to aviation and space research projects and was selected as an astronaut in April 1966.

After serving in support and backup roles for the Apollo IX and X missions, he piloted the lunar module on Apollo XIV, for man's third moon landing in February 1971. The mission returned a record 100 pounds of lunar samples to earth and achieved several notable "firsts" in space flight.

Mitchell retired from the U.S. Navy in the grade of captain with 5,000 hours flying time, almost 217 of them in space. He was awarded the Presidential Medal of Freedom in 1970.

JOE L. MORGAN

In twenty-two seasons in major league baseball between 1965 and his retirement in 1983, Joe Morgan played in a total of 2,649 games, winning the National League's Most Valuable Player Award in 1975 and again in 1976. He was born in Bonham on September 19, 1943.

During his career, Morgan's 2,517 hits included 1,704 single base hits, 449 doubles, ninety-six triples and 268 home runs. He led the National League in 1976 with a batting average of .320, scoring 113 runs and batting in another 111.

Morgan's value as a player was reflected in the demand for his skills. He played first for the Houston Astros, then for the Cincinnati Reds, where he helped beat the Boston Red Sox in the 1975 World Series with a single with bases loaded in the tenth inning.

Morgan returned to the Houston Astros in 1980, then ended his career with the San Francisco Giants, Philadelphia Phillies and Oakland Athletics before retiring in 1983 at the age of forty.

AUDIE MURPHY

The most highly-decorated American soldier in World War II, Audie Murphy was awarded a total of twenty-eight United States and foreign medals for valor, including the Congressional Medal of Honor. Born in Kingston on June 20, 1924, he fought in Tunisia, Italy, France and Germany and was awarded a battlefield commission in October 1944.

On January 26, 1945, with only eighteen men in his command, Murphy held off six German tanks and more than 200 infantry, calling for artillery support to within fifty yards of his position. He was awarded the Medal of Honor on June 2, 1945.

After the war, he acted in more than two dozen films, including *The Red Badge of Courage* and *To Hell and Back*, based on his own wartime experiences. He was killed in an aircraft accident near Galax, Virginia, on May 28, 1971, at the age of forty-six.

His uniforms, medals and mementos are preserved in the Audie Murphy Room at the Walworth Harrison Public Library on Lee Street in Greenville.

WILLIE NELSON

A superstar for more than two decades, Willie Nelson learned to play guitar as a child and started playing in honky tonk and Czech polka bands as a teenager.

He was born in Abbott on April 30, 1933. After serving in the U.S. Air Force in Korea, he became a disc jockey in Waco, then was featured on his own daytime country music show in Fort Worth, while writing and selling songs for a few hundred dollars each.

In 1960, he moved to Nashville, where he recorded hits such as "Funny How Time Slips Away," "Hello Walls," and "Crazy." He recorded eighteen albums for RCA, starting in 1964 and including "Texas in My Soul," "Yesterday's Wine," and "The Words Don't Fit the Picture." When his house in Tennessee burned in 1971, he moved back to Texas and organized a number of outdoor concerts.

His major albums in the 1980s included "Once More with Feeling," "Always on My Mind," "Good Hearted Woman," "The Promiseland," and "Master of Suspense."

Ever a flamboyant personality, Nelson works hard and plays hard. His deep concern for the plight of farmers is reflected in his several Farm Aid benefit performances.

CHESTER WILLIAM NIMITZ

When Japan surrendered at the end of World War II on September 2, 1945, the ceremony took place on the deck of the *USS Missouri*, flagship of Admiral of the Fleet Chester W. Nimitz.

Nimitz was born on February 24, 1885, in Fredericksburg. After his graduation from the U.S. Naval Academy in 1905, he served as a submarine officer aboard *Plunger* and *Skipjack*. He rose rapidly in the Navy and was promoted to rear admiral in 1938 in command of a cruiser division, then a battleship division. In December 1941, he was promoted to admiral in command of the U.S. Pacific Fleet, directing U.S. victories in the battles of Midway, the Philippine Sea and Leyte Gulf.

From December 1945 until his retirement in December 1947, Admiral Nimitz served as chief of naval operations; until 1949, he was a special assistant to the secretary of the navy. He died in California on February 20, 1966.

The Admiral Nimitz State Historical Park and Museum are located on the grounds of his grandfather's Nimitz Hotel in Fredericksburg.

BILL PICKETT

A legendary cowboy and rodeo performer, Bill Pickett is credited with the introduction of a new event to the rodeo: bulldogging. He'd been bringing steers to ground by biting their lips or noses for at least a decade before he did so in a rodeo in 1908. Bulldogging soon became a popular event.

Pickett was born in Jenks-Branch on December 5, 1870, and was employed at the giant 101 Ranch in Oklahoma most of his working life. The ranch toured its own rodeo and wild west show throughout the United States, with Pickett by 1912 billed as the Dusky Demon, performing his bulldogging feats in twenty-two states as many as 400 times a year.

He semi-retired to his own small ranch near Chandler, Oklahoma, in 1916 but continued to work and perform from time to time for the 101 Ranch. He died on April 2, 1932, as the result of an accident while rounding up horses.

Pickett was elected to the National Rodeo Cowboy Hall of Fame in 1971, the twentieth such honoree and the first black cowboy so honored.

WILLIAM SYDNEY PORTER

After two years on a sheep ranch in South Texas, where he'd moved for his health, William Sydney Porter (1862-1910) moved to Austin in 1884. The first three years he took a succession of odd jobs, but, after his marriage to Athol Estes in 1887, he settled down as a teller for the First National Bank of Austin.

Continuing to write in his spare time, he left Austin for a job on a Houston newspaper in 1895, but he was indicted eight months later for embezzling from his former employer. Wrongly convicted, he served a prison sentence from 1898 to 1901. Because his wife had died in 1897, he moved to New York when released and continued to write with great success under the pseudonym "O. Henry" until his death.

He published nearly 400 short stories, including such classics as "The Gift of the Magi" and "The Ransom of Red Chief," with some forty stories having Texas settings.

His former residence at 409 East Fifth Street in Austin has been preserved and is open to the public five days a week.

WILEY POST

One of the featured exhibits at the National Air and Space Museum in Washington, D.C., is a Lockheed Vega aircraft in which Wiley Post won the Bendix Trophy in 1930, then flew around the world in a record eight days, fifteen hours and fifty-one minutes. The aircraft is the legendary *Winnie Mae*.

Wiley Post was born in Grand Saline on November 22, 1899. As a teenager, he saw his first airplane and was consumed by a love of flying thereafter. Following his 1930 record flight around the world with Harold Getty as his navigator, he repeated the feat alone in 1933 to demonstrate high altitude and flight instrument technology. He also set an unofficial altitude record of 49,000 feet, wearing a pressurized flight suit, the following year.

At the height of his fame, he set out with his friend, humorist Will Rogers, in August 1935 to fly to the Orient by way of Alaska. Fifteen miles south of Point Barrow, their aircraft crashed after take-off, killing them both.

RANDY QUAID

In twenty appearances during the first fourteen years of his career, Randy Quaid received one Oscar and two Emmy nominations for his work in motion pictures and television.

Born in Houston on October 1, 1950, he developed an interest in acting at Bellaire High School, Houston Baptist College and the University of Houston. Director Peter Bogdanovich was impressed with his work in amateur productions and cast him in several of his early films, including *Targets, The Last Picture Show, Paper Moon* and *What's Up, Doc?* His Oscar nomination in 1973 was for his supporting role in *The Last Detail*, with Jack Nicholson.

Other memorable motion picture roles were in *The Missouri Breaks, Midnight Express, Caddyshack II,* and *National Lampoon's Vacation.*

Quaid has also appeared on stage with his brother, Dennis Quaid, and on film with him in *The Long Riders.* From 1985 to 1986 he also spent a season on television's "Saturday Night Live." He had his own short-lived television series, "Davis Rules," in the 1990-1991 and 1991-1992 seasons.

SAMUEL T. RAYBURN

Educated in a rural one-room schoolhouse, Sam Rayburn (1882-1961) worked his way through East Texas State University, then earned his law degree from the University of Texas and was admitted to the bar in 1908.

He served in the Texas Legislature from 1907 to 1913, the last two years as Speaker of the House. In 1912, he won election to the U.S. Congress, serving until his death in 1961, a total of more than forty-eight years. In 1940, he was elected Speaker of the House, a post he held for the rest of his life, except for four years when the Democratic Party was in the minority. He was a trusted advisor to Presidents Roosevelt, Truman, Eisenhower and Kennedy, and instrumental in the passage of important New Deal legislation.

The Rayburn House Office Building on Capitol Hill in Washington is named in his honor, and the Sam Rayburn House and Museum and Sam Rayburn Library, both in Bonham, open to the public daily, keep "Mister Sam's" memory alive in Texas.

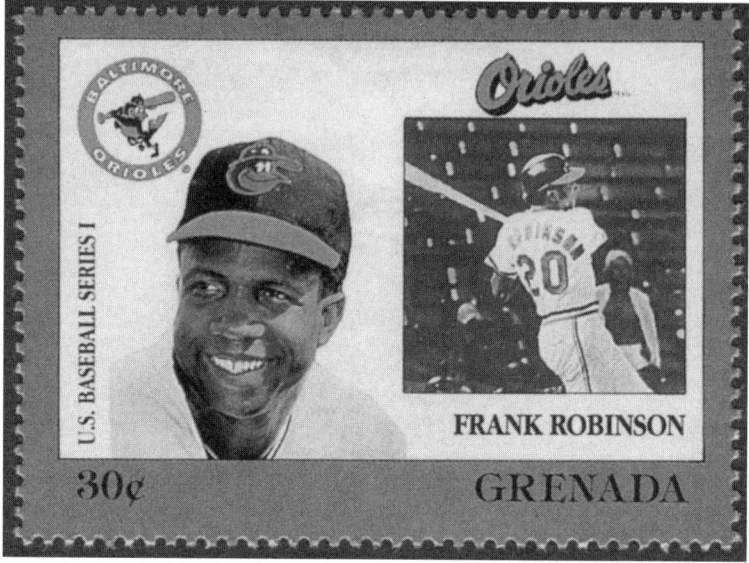

FRANK ROBINSON

The only baseball player ever to win Most Valuable Player titles in both the American and National leagues, Frank Robinson did so in the National League in 1961 with the Cincinnati Reds. After he was traded to the Baltimore Orioles in 1966, he hit forty-nine home runs, scored 122 runs and recorded a .323 batting average to earn the same title in the American League.

Robinson was born in Beaumont on August 31, 1935, became a professional baseball player at age twenty-one and, after hitting twenty-one home runs that season, was named National League Rookie of the Year.

In 1973, Robinson was traded to the California Angels as a designated hitter, then played a season for the Cleveland Indians, before being appointed the first African-American manager in major league baseball with the Cleveland Indians in 1975. He went on to manage the San Francisco Giants and the Baltimore Orioles between 1981 and 1991. He was elected to the Baseball Hall of Fame in his first year of eligibility.

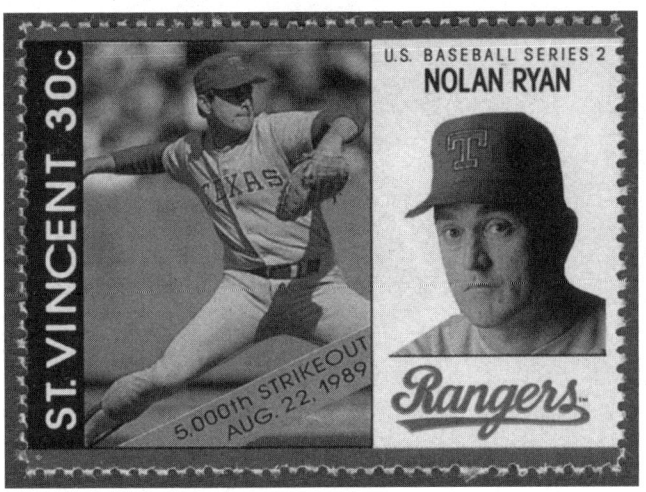

NOLAN RYAN

In twenty-three major-league seasons, Nolan Ryan established himself as one of baseball's all-time great pitchers. Born in Refugio on January 31, 1947, he played first for the New York Mets for four seasons and was traded to the California Angels in 1971. He became a star there, pitching a fastball clocked at more than 100 miles an hour. He was 19-6 in his first season, leading the league with nine shutouts and 329 strikeouts.

He led the American League in strikeouts four years, starting in 1976. Traded to the Houston Astros in 1980, he continued to set pitching records in 1987 and 1988. In 1989, he joined the Texas Rangers and led the American League in strikeouts in 1989 and 1990 with 301 and 232 respectively.

Troubled by injuries, Ryan elected to retire after the 1993 season but, even at age forty-six, was able to deliver a ninety-six mile-per-hour fastball and pitch a seventh no-hitter, shattering Sandy Koufax's career record of four.

Ryan has been elected to the Texas Sports Hall of Fame and is eligible to enter the Baseball Hall of Fame in 1998.

DAVID R. SCOTT

As commander of Apollo XIII, astronaut David R. Scott participated in the first extended exploration of the moon utilizing the lunar roving vehicle. He'd previously flown on the Gemini VIII and Apollo IX missions.

Born in San Antonio on June 6, 1932, he graduated from the United States Military Academy in 1954 and received advanced degrees in aeronautics and astronautics from the Massachusetts Institute of Technology.

On the Gemini VIII mission in 1966, he and fellow astronaut Neil Armstrong performed the first successful docking of two vehicles in space.

A former test pilot, Scott retired from the United States Air Force as a colonel in 1975 with 5,600 hours flying time, almost 547 of them in space flight. He is a recipient of the Collier Trophy, Schilling Trophy, Federation Aeronautique Gold Medal, United Nations Peace Medal and numerous NASA and Air Force decorations.

ELLIOT M. SEE, JR.

Selected by NASA for its astronaut training program in September 1962, Elliot M. See, Jr., participated in every phase of training until he was chosen as backup pilot for the Gemini V flight and command pilot for the Gemini IX mission.

He was born in Dallas on July 23, 1927. After his graduation from the United States Merchant Marine Academy and receipt of an advanced degree in engineering from the University of California at Los Angeles, he served as a naval aviator from 1953 to 1956.

When See was selected for the astronaut program, he had logged more than 3,300 hours in jet aircraft, much of it as a test pilot. He was selected as the command pilot for Gemini IX.

Captain See and his fellow astronaut, Major Charles A. Bassett, died on February 28, 1966, during an accident while making an instrument landing at St. Louis, Missouri.

ANN SHERIDAN

A beauty contest winner at the age of eighteen, actress Ann Sheridan was placed under contract in 1933 by Paramount Pictures, which promoted her career as "The Oomph Girl." She was born in Denton on February 21, 1915.

After playing small parts for a couple of years, she landed her first leading role in *Rocky Mountain Mystery*, a western whodunit, in 1935.

Paramount kept her busy in supporting roles until she signed with Warner Brothers in 1936. In 1937, she was cast with Pat O'Brien and Humphrey Bogart in *The Great O'Malley*, the film which established her as a leading lady.

She continued to star in major productions throughout the 1940s, including *Angels With Dirty Faces, Dodge City, They Drive by Night* and *The Man Who Came to Dinner*. Critics agreed her finest performance was as a small-town girl in *King's Row*.

Prior to her death of cancer on January 21, 1967, she starred in two television series.

TOMMIE C. SMITH

In just four years of competition, track star Tommie C. Smith set a total of seven world records, two of them on June 11, 1966, in the 200-yard and 200-meter events.

Born in Clarksville on June 5, 1944, Smith played football and basketball at San Jose State University but decided to focus on track in his junior year. He won NCAA and AAU events in 1967 and 1968 and set world records of 44.5 seconds in the 400-meter and 44.8 in the 440-yard dashes.

In the 1968 Olympic Games in Mexico City, he set a new world record of 19.83 seconds in the 200-meter, despite being wrapped in tape for a pulled groin muscle.

He returned to college, graduating from San Jose State University in 1969, whereupon he joined the Cincinnati Bengals as a wide receiver for three seasons. He later became athletic director and track coach at Oberlin College in Ohio. Since 1978, he has been track and cross country coach at Santa Monica College in southern California.

ERNEST TUBB

One of the greatest performers of country music who achieved fame playing Jimmie Rodgers' original guitar, Ernest Tubb headlined the first country music concert at Carnegie Hall in 1947.

Born in Crisp on February 9, 1914, Tubb got his start as a musician on radio in San Antonio on KONO, then in Fort Worth on KGKO, where he soon attained recognition in 1942 as the "Texas Troubador." One of the first musicians to play an electric guitar, Tubb became a regular soloist at the Grand Old Opry in Nashville, performing a fusion of honky-tonk melodies, country vocals and western swing.

His major recordings included "I'm Walking the Floor Over You," "Goodnight Irene," "Hey, Mr. Bluebird," "No Help Wanted," and "Throw Your Love My Way." Between 1942 and 1947, Tubb appeared in several motion pictures with Bing Crosby and Charles Starrett.

Ernest Tubb died in Nashville, Tennessee, on September 6, 1984, at the age of seventy.

TANYA TUCKER

She was only thirteen years of age, the youngest of three children of a construction worker, when Tanya Tucker began her career as a country music singer. Born in Seminole on October 10, 1958, she grew up in Texas, Arizona, Utah and Nevada—wherever her father's work took the family.

Her parents encouraged her vocal efforts and helped her get a small part in a motion picture. After she'd cut a demonstration tape, she and her father went to Nashville in March 1972 for her first recording session. While she was still a teenager, her "Delta Dawn" became a major success, one of the bestselling albums of the year.

She went on to record numerous top ten country hits in the 1970s and 1980s, including "Jamestown Ferry," "Texas: When I Die," "Pecos Promenade," "Can I See You Tonight?" and "San Antonio Stroll."

EDWARD H. WHITE II

The first man to "walk" in space, Edward H. White II, spent twenty-three minutes outside the Gemini IV spacecraft in June 1965. Born in San Antonio on November 14, 1930, the son of an Air Force officer, he was a 1952 graduate of the United States Military Academy and recipient of advanced degrees in aeronautics and astronautics from the University of Michigan.

During his Air Force service, he was a fighter pilot and test pilot until selected as an astronaut by NASA in September 1962. Subsequent to his four-day space flight as pilot of Gemini IV, Lieutenant Colonel White was named senior pilot for the first mission in the Apollo program.

He and fellow astronauts Gus Grissom and Roger Chaffee died on January 27, 1967, at Cape Kennedy, Florida, when a flash fire consumed their spacecraft during a simulated launch.

The Edward H. White II Memorial Museum, housed in the Air Force's sole remaining World War I hangar at Brooks Air Force Base, San Antonio, is named in his honor.

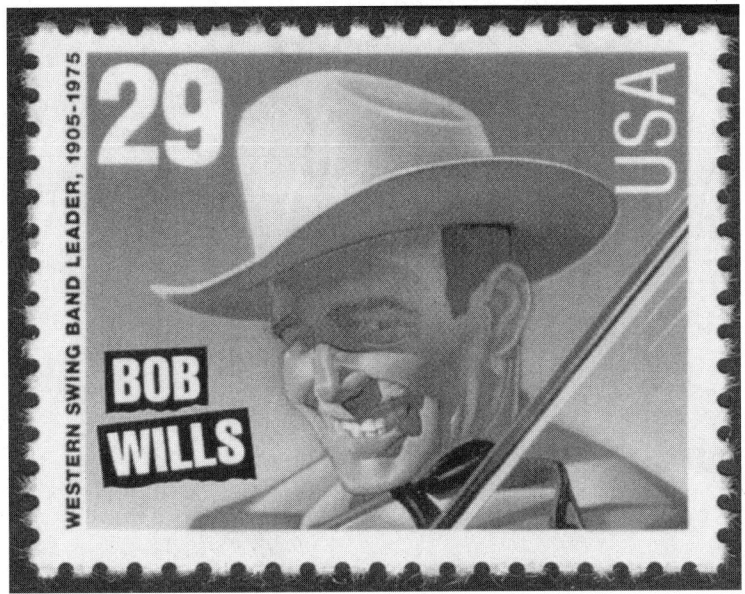

BOB WILLS

Like his grandfather, father and several uncles, James Robert Wills was an outstanding fiddler, highly regarded for his improvisation. Born in Kosse on March 6, 1905, he was still breaking attendance records at live concerts in his mid-sixties. His 1939 recording of "San Antonio Rose" sold over a million copies, extraordinary at that time. It is regarded as consummate Bob Wills and pure Texas.

By the 1940s, he was recognized as the undisputed King of Western Swing. Groups he headed during his career were the Aladdin Laddies, Light Crust Doughboys and, with great success, the Texas Playboys. By 1943, he had headed a twenty-two-piece orchestra in California and appeared in thirteen feature films, including *Take Me Back to Oklahoma* and *Go West Young Lady* with Glen Ford and Ann Miller.

Bob Wills died in Fort Worth on May 13, 1975. The Bob Wills Museum at Turkey in Hall County contains memorabilia of the Texas Playboys and Wills' influence on American music.

MILDRED DIDRIKSON ZAHARIAS

Likely the greatest woman athlete of all time, Mildred "Babe" Didrikson Zaharias, won two gold medals and a silver medal at the 1932 Olympic Games in track and field events.

Born in Port Arthur on June 26, 1914, she played basketball, tennis and swam, but, after her Olympic victories, she discovered golf. As an amateur, she captured seventeen tournaments in a row. Then, during the first six years of the Ladies Professional Golf Association (LPGA) she posted twenty-four wins and was the top LPGA money-winner four years in a row. During her career, she won a total of eighty-two tournaments in all.

In 1938, Mildred "Babe" Didrikson married professional wrestler George Zaharias. In 1949, the Associated Press named her "outstanding woman athlete of the half century."

Mildred "Babe" Zaharias lost her battle against cancer at the age of forty-eight on September 27, 1956. The people of Beaumont, where she was raised, have erected a museum and memorial in her memory on King Parkway.

LONE STAR LOCALES

American Quarter Horse Heritage Center

No breed of horse is more popular or numerous than the versatile American Quarter Horse. The American Quarter Horse Association (AQHA), with headquarters in Amarillo has 277,000 members in seventy-seven countries worldwide, carries 3.2 million horses on its registry and sanctions some 2,300 shows annually.

Agile and intelligent, these horses were prized during the open range and trail driving era in the late-nineteenth century and helped explore the vast frontier. The name is a tribute to the horse's speed at a quarter-mile distance, of special value to generations of cowboys who worked cattle on the open ranges of Texas. The quarter horse is characterized by a broad head, large eyes, sensitive nostrils, strong jaws and a wide, deep chest.

The spacious American Quarter Horse Heritage Center and Museum in Amarillo boasts galleries devoted to the breed's history, grooming and care. And, of course, a stable with a number of these magnificent horses visitors may ride.

American Ex-Prisoners of War

In two world wars, the Korean and Vietnam conflicts and other military actions, 142,257 American military personnel have been captured and interned as prisoners of war. Of these, 17,034 died in captivity, while 125,202 eventually were returned to U.S. military control.

At the beginning of 1995, of the 62,676 still alive, an impressive total of more than 34,000, or over fifty-five percent, were active members of American Ex-Prisoners of War, Inc., with national headquarters in Arlington. The organization was established in April 1942 following the fall of the Bataan Peninsula.

With chapters in most states, the organization publishes a monthly bulletin and holds an annual convention in September each year. Various committees are dedicated to the study of malnutrition and starvation of prisoners of war, legislation, military history, surviving spouses and liaison with the Department of Defense and Department of Veterans Affairs.

AUSTIN

National Wildflower Research Center

Native wildflowers, once considered undesirable and unattractive, have captured the interest and affection of Texans as never before, thanks in large degree to the efforts of Lady Bird Johnson, widow of President Lyndon B. Johnson. The National Wildflower Research Center was founded by Mrs. Johnson in 1982.

Because a variety of climates and soils can be found in Texas, some 5,400 plant varieties with 462 species, subspecies and varieties are endemic to the Lone Star State.

In April 1995, with the dedication of the National Wildflower Research Center ten miles southwest of Austin, the preservation and re-establishment of native flora has attained new importance. The forty-two-acre facility, with eight buildings, attracts some 100,000 visitors each year.

For over sixty years, the Texas Department of Transportation has beautified more than 700,000 acres of highway right-of-way by planting literally tons of wildflower seeds annually.

Aransas National Wildlife Refuge

When the Aransas National Wildlife Refuge on San Antonio Bay at Austwell, some forty-eight miles northeast of Corpus Christi, was created in 1938, a mere eighteen whooping cranes wintered there. By 1993, more than ninety of these endangered birds made the journey every October from their warm-weather habitat at the Wood Buffalo National Park in the Canadian province of Alberta to spend the winter months in Texas.

The Aransas National Wildlife Refuge is extraordinarily visitor-friendly, with a sixteen-mile paved loop from which wildlife viewing and photo opportunities abound, plus walking trails and an observation tower.

In addition to whooping cranes, about 300 other species of birds, white-tailed deer, raccoons, javelina and nine-banded armadillos are indigenous to the refuge.

The Aransas National Wildlife Refuge is open to the public daily from 8 A.M. to 5 P.M.

LAKE BUCHANAN
American Bald Eagles

When the American bald eagle was first classified as an endangered species in 1967, biologists feared that only a few hundred might still survive in the wilderness.

However, twenty-five years later, more than 1,000 are observed annually wintering at twenty-two habitats in Texas, such as those in the Lake Buchanan region. They come every year from as far away as Canada and Alaska, attracted by fish and waterfowl prey.

The most noble symbol of the nation, the American eagle is not "bald" but features snowy feathers on its head and tail after its third year. It wasn't until June 20, 1782, after a six-year debate in the Continental Congress, that the American bald eagle became the nation's national emblem. Surprisingly, that otherwise shrewd founding father, Benjamin Franklin, opposed the choice, arguing that the wild turkey was "a true native of America."

The Texas Wildlife and Parks Department conducts a bald eagle survey every January at East Texas reservoirs, along the Guadalupe and Llano rivers and in remote canyons, with the assistance of dozens of volunteers.

CLEAR LAKE

Lyndon B. Johnson Space Center

Situated on a 1,620-acre site, twenty-five miles southeast of downtown Houston, the Lyndon B. Johnson Space Center is known worldwide as "mission control" for all U.S. manned space flights. Much of the land on which it was built was contributed by Rice University.

The Space Center opened officially in September 1963, a little more than two years after President John F. Kennedy challenged the nation to send men to the moon. Originally named the Manned Spacecraft Center, it was renamed in honor of the late Lyndon B. Johnson in February 1973.

Its principal functions include the design of advanced spacecraft, astronaut training and space flight planning and monitoring. The center's director reports to the National Aeronautics and Space Administration in Washington, D.C.

A substantial visitor center contains 50,000 square feet of display area and an 800-seat auditorium. Much of the facility is open to the public from 9 A.M. to 4 P.M. daily except on Christmas Day.

Columbus Fleet

In 1992, the world celebrated the 500th anniversary of the first voyage of Christopher Columbus to the New World. He set sail from Palos, Spain, on August 2, 1492, in command of three vessels, the *Niña*, *Pinta* and *Santa Maria* under the patronage of King Ferdinand and Queen Isabella of Spain. Columbus made his first landfall in the New World on October 11.

In recognition of his discoveries, the government of Spain built authentic replicas of his three vessels, sailed them across the North Atlantic, then contributed them to the City of Corpus Christi on a fifty-year loan as an historical exhibit.

The *Niña*, *Pinta* and *Santa Maria* replicas are anchored at Cargo Dock One in Corpus Christi's harbor and open to the public daily from 10 A.M. to 5 P.M., except for Christmas Day. A nearby museum features exhibits of artifacts recovered from Spanish treasure ships lost to storms in the Caribbean during two centuries.

CORPUS CHRISTI

International Kite Museum

The International Kite Museum, hard by a breezy beach in Corpus Christi, is one of only two kite museums in the United States. The other is the World Kite Museum and Hall of Fame in Long Beach, Washington. Others may be found in Japan and India.

The Texas museum's exhibits highlight Chinese military and ceremonial kites, those used by scientists such as Benjamin Franklin, the Wright brothers, Guglielmo Marconi, who used kites to carry antennas aloft, and Texan Samuel Cody, who received the first patent for a man-lifting kite in England in 1901.

The museum's displays were prepared with the assistance of the Smithsonian Institution, National Oceanic and Atmospheric Administration and the Library of Congress.

A visit to the museum, besides being instructive, can also be fun. Numerous varieties of kites are available in its well-stocked gift shop, and there's that splendid beach with a steady breeze outside.

CORPUS CHRISTI

USS Lexington (CV-16)

Today a floating museum of naval history on the bay in Corpus Christi, the *USS Lexington* (CV-16) served the United States longer and set more records than any other aircraft carrier in the history of naval aviation.

She was launched September 26, 1942, and named for her predecessor, the *USS Lexington* (CV-2), which had been lost in the Battle of the Coral Sea four months earlier.

During World War II, she spent twenty-one months in combat in the Pacific. Her aircraft destroyed 372 enemy planes in the air and another 475 on the ground. Her aircraft sank more than 300,000 tons of enemy shipping. The *USS Lexington* was reported sunk by the Japanese no less than four times. Her distinctive blue color, rather than camouflage, contributed to the nickname by which her adversaries knew her, the "blue ghost."

The *USS Lexington* was decommissioned in November 1991. She's open to the public daily from 9 A.M. to 5 P.M., except on Christmas Day.

CORPUS CHRISTI
Texas State Aquarium

The Gulf of Mexico teems with marine life and the Texas State Aquarium in Corpus Christi, with its unique North American coral reefs, offers visitors an opportunity to view more than 250 species in marine habitats. Some 350,000 gallons of sea water are recirculated every day.

Tarpon, sharks, eels, as well as angelfish, mackerel, and tiny damselfish dart back and forth around artificial coral reefs. The aquarium contains several exhibits in order to show estuary, bay, salt marsh and deep-water marine environments. Visitors often get a close-up view whenever volunteers hand feed some of the species.

The Texas State Aquarium is located on Corpus Christi Beach, across the city's ship channel from several museums and other visitor attractions but is served by a shuttle bus and water taxi.

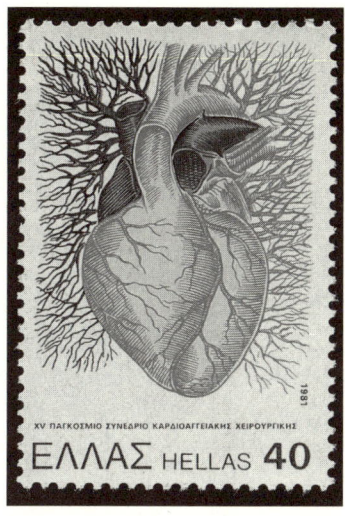

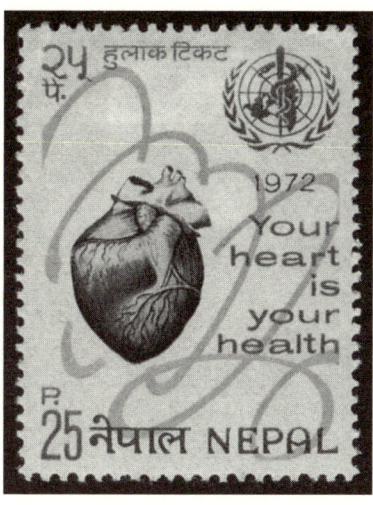

DALLAS
American Heart Association

One of the nation's foremost health organizations, the American Heart Association (AHA) relocated its national headquarters from New York City to Dallas in 1975.

Founded in 1924, it disburses more than $230 million each year on scientific research, public and professional education and community programs. In addition to its various scientific journals and bulletins, the AHA also publishes several cookbooks and conducts nutritional programs for consumers.

The American Heart Association has some 2,100 branches, divisions and affiliates in all fifty states, with more than four million volunteers assisting 25,000 health-care professionals who provide medical direction.

Sometimes referred to as the "Heart Fund," the AHA depends on public support in the form of contributions, bequests and special events. Its emphasis is on research and education to combat heart disease and strokes, two of the nation's leading causes of death.

Helium Field Operations

The seat of Moore County, Dumas is located close to the center of vast helium-bearing natural gas fields which stretch from the Texas Panhandle, across the Oklahoma Panhandle and into Kansas. About seventy-five percent of the nation's helium reserves are located there, enabling the United States to produce ninety percent of the world's supply.

The most visible use for helium is in lighter-than-air dirigibles and blimps, for which it has been used in U.S. airships since 1921. It is an inert gas and far safer than hydrogen, which is easily flammable. In fact, helium is the most chemically inert substance known, as well as being colorless, odorless, tasteless and non-toxic.

Helium has numerous other uses, some less known. It is used in cryogenics, arc welding, as a manufacturing quality control agent, in deep sea diving and magnetic resonance imaging.

U.S. production and storage is managed by the U.S. Bureau of Mines, which maintains Helium Field Operations headquarters in Amarillo.

EL PASO
Fort Bliss

In September 1849, less than four years after Texas attained statehood, United States troops arrived on the Rio Grande to establish Fort Bliss at what would become the city of El Paso, across the river from Juárez, Mexico.

The post was relocated several times but has occupied its present site continuously since October 1893. A number of its original buildings are still in use.

Fort Bliss was a cavalry post until early in World War II when it became an artillery base. Later, captured German rockets were brought there for study, and the first American military rocket was tested there. Fort Bliss was designated as the U.S. Army's Air Defense Center in 1957.

Today, there are four museums at Fort Bliss and nearby Biggs Army Airfield: the Fort Bliss Museum, Third Cavalry Museum, Air Defense & Artillery Museum and the Museum of the Noncommissioned Officer. All are open to the public weekdays without charge.

Western American Art

Situated in the city's cultural district, Fort Worth's Amon Carter Museum is noted for its exceptional collection of western American art, notably works by Frederic Remington (1861-1909) and Charles M. Russell (1864-1926).

The museum was founded by newspaper publisher and philanthropist Amon G. Carter, Sr., who collected paintings and sculpture by leading artists of the American West. The museum was designed by architect Philip Johnson. Since its opening in 1961, it has had two additions, in 1964 and 1977.

Today the museum's collection includes seventy works by Remington and 350 by Russell, with two galleries devoted exclusively to their work. Other prominent American artists whose works are held by the museum include George Catlin, Thomas Cole, Childe Hassam, Winslow Homer and Georgia O'Keeffe. The average number of annual visitors tops 135,000.

An additional fifty-five paintings by Remington and Russell may be seen at the Sid Richardson Collection of Western Art in downtown Fort Worth's historic Sundance Square.

GALVESTON

Historic Landmark Districts

No city in Texas can claim as many historic buildings as Galveston. By one account, the city has 550 structures listed on the National Register of Historic Places, most of them situated in the East End National Historic Landmark District and the Silk Stocking Historic District.

Many are elegantly restored mansions built in the mid-nineteenth century by wealthy entrepreneurs and merchants. Others are historic churches and, along the Strand, iron-front commercial buildings. Distinctive brown street signs identify the city's historic districts, and maps of walking tours are available at the Strand Visitors Center.

Noteworthy public buildings depicted on United States postcards are the Old Galveston Customs House and Court House, a Greek Revival red brick building completed in 1861, and the Ashbel Smith Building, in Romanesque style, completed in 1900. It is still used as originally intended by the University of Texas Medical School. Restored in 1984, it's referred to by students and faculty by its nickname, "Old Red."

GLEN ROSE
Dinosaur Valley State Park

Tyrannosaurus, Euplocephalus, Acrocanthosaurus and Pleurocelus were dinosaurs who roamed the southwest between 225 and sixty-five million years ago during the Mesozoic Era. Paleontologists have identified some 350 different dinosaur types.

Texas is rich in evidence of the era and one of few states able to dedicate an entire park to the Mesozoic Era. Dinosaur Valley State Park, five miles west of Glen Rose on the Paluxy River, is the site of numerous dinosaur footprints, first discovered in 1912.

The Texas Parks and Wildlife Department purchased the 1,270-acre property in 1969 and opened it to the public the following year. A visitor center provides information about the geology of the area and the dinosaurs who inhabited the region.

A prominent feature are the two life-size fiberglass dinosaurs retired following the 1964 New York World's Fair. There are also six camping sites along the park's five miles of hiking trails.

Fossil Rim Wildlife Center

Texas' landscape and climate have proven hospitable to wildlife from other continents, notably Africa. In fact, there are almost a dozen exotic wildlife sanctuaries in Texas, more than in any other state.

With 3,000 acres, the Fossil Rim Wildlife Center near Glen Rose is by far the largest. Home to 1,100 free roaming animals from around the world, it is much more than a visitor attraction.

Fossil Rim is also part of a global network of conservation organizations preserving endangered species. Here one can see both the black and white rhinoceros, giraffes, zebras, African addax antelopes, cheetahs and other exotic species as well as deer, wolves, ostriches and native American fowl.

Fossil Rim Wildlife Center offers non-invasive habitat tours and camera safaris year-round except on Christmas Day and Thanksgiving Day, either along its scenic drive or, for a closer look, guided, behind-the-scenes and conservation tours, accompanied by naturalist guides.

Marine Military Academy

The Marine Military Academy is the only college preparatory school in the country which adheres to the customs and traditions of the U.S. Marine Corps. It has an enrollment of 530 students in grades eight through twelve, plus a postgraduate year.

Prominent on the Iwo Jima Road campus in Harlingen is the original working model of the U.S. Marine Corps Memorial at Arlington National Cemetery, donated to the academy by its sculptor, Felix W. de Weldon. A visitor center and museum are nearby.

Of the five U.S. Marines depicted raising the flag atop Mount Suribachi, Iwo Jima, one was a native Texan. Corporal Harlon H. Block was born in Yorktown and raised in Weslaco. He is the Marine shown planting the base of the flagpole in photographer Joe Rosenthal's Pulitzer Prize photograph which inspired the sculpture. Corporal Block later died in action on Iwo Jima and is buried in Weslaco. An abstract sculpture in his memory in Harlon Block Memorial Park at Seventh and Bridge Streets in Weslaco was dedicated in 1977.

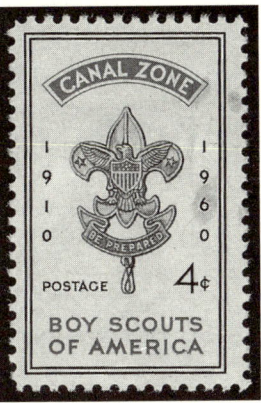

Boy Scouts of America

After more than twenty-five years in New Jersey, the Boy Scouts of America (BSA) relocated its national headquarters to Irving in 1979.

Total membership since its founding in 1910, with President William Howard Taft as honorary president, totals more than ninety million. Current youth membership stands at slightly more than four million, with a million adult leaders. The BSA has 129,600 packs, troops, posts and other units administered by 355 local councils.

The national headquarters publishes three magazines for various levels of BSA members: *Boy's Life, Exploring,* and *Scouting,* as well as handbooks, pamphlets, training programs and other literature.

In 1993, scouting organizers in several countries of the former Soviet Union turned to the Boy Scouts of America for help. In response, the BSA produced 20,000 copies of the first *Russian Scout Handbook* for distribution in their countries.

IRVING

Mothers Against Drunk Driving

Mothers Against Drunk Driving (MADD) was founded in Fair Oaks, California, in 1980 by a mother whose thirteen-year-old daughter was killed by a hit-and-run repeat offender. It has grown since as a national organization with 500 local chapters, community action teams and state offices. Today, it has over three million members and supporters.

MADD relocated its national headquarters to Hurst, Texas, in 1983, then to Irving in July 1990, where a professional staff of fifty, assisted by numerous volunteers, directs its national programs. These include public awareness, especially prior to and during major holidays, legislative action and victim services. MADD monitors legislation, sponsors competitions and awards, public service announcements and fund-raising events.

The U.S. Department of Transportation estimates that, of 40,676 annual traffic fatalities in the United States, some 16,489, or 40.8 percent, are alcohol-related.

JACKSBORO
Head, Heart, Hands and Health

When journalist and agriculture agent Tom Marks tried to help local farmers improve their crops in 1907, he met with an overwhelming lack of interest. Undeterred, he organized their sons the following year into the Jacksboro Boys Corn Club and produced a successful fair. His idea inspired the formation of similar clubs around Texas and attracted the attention of state and federal officials.

Thus developed in Jack County a concept recognized when Congress passed the Smith-Lever Act in 1914, formalizing the 4-H movement. Today, 3,500,000 boys and girls participate in 4-H clubs in every state, under the guidance of 400,000 adult leaders. The movement spread to Canada in 1931 and since then to some eighty other countries.

Tom Marks' home, built in 1882, now houses the Jack County Museum, in which an entire room is devoted to the history of the 4-H movement.

KERRVILLE

U. S. Army Camel Corps

Camp Verde, twelve miles south of Kerrville, was the site of an unusual experiment in military transport. In April 1856, the United States Army had imported thirty-four camels from North Africa, followed by an additional forty-one the following year. Another eighty-one followed in 1861, some of them making they way to Verde. The experiment, authorized by Jefferson Davis, when he was secretary of war, was highly successful. The camels passed every test. They carried heavier loads than mules and needed less water and would forage on virtually any plant.

The U. S. Army built a large camel corral at Camp Verde. During the Civil War when Confederate troops occupied Camp Verde they continued to use the beasts. Camels might have become the preferred form of transport on the frontier but for their contrary nature and foul odor. After the war Union troops reoccupied Camp Verde and promptly got rid of the animals, selling off some and turning others loose to fend for themselves in the Texas Hill County.

Camp Verde was abandoned in 1869.

LA PORTE

USS Texas (BB-35)

The only surviving naval vessel to have served with the fleet in both World War I and World War II, the *USS Texas* (BB-35) was decommissioned in 1948 and presented to the people of Texas. She is berthed at the San Jacinto Battlefield, twenty-two miles east of Houston. She was designated a national historic landmark in 1977 and has been operated by the Texas Parks and Wildlife Department since 1983 as a memorial museum. The vessel is open to the public seven days a week. Extensive restoration was completed in July 1990.

Commissioned in 1914, she saw thirty-two years of service, starting with the U.S. landing at Veracruz, Mexico, in 1914. In 1919, the *USS Texas* became the first battleship to launch an aircraft. In World War II, she spent 362 days on patrol and convoy duty and 116 days in actual combat. Her big guns supported the Allied landings in North Africa, Normandy, southern France, Iwo Jima and Okinawa.

Pan American Highway

A short drive across the International Bridge at Laredo marks the beginning of the 3,350-mile Inter-American Highway to Panama. This highway is but one part of a larger system, the Pan American Highway, which, with connecting routes, links every country in Latin America and seventeen of its capital cities. Its total length is more than 45,000 miles.

Segments of the Pan American Highway pass through every imaginable type of terrain and climate, from dense jungles and deserts to cold mountain passes as high as 15,000 feet. From Caracas, Venezuela, south along the coast, one section of the Pan American Highway as far as Quito, Ecuador, is also known as the Simon Bolívar Highway.

The first Pan American Highway Congress to plan and develop road systems throughout the Western Hemisphere met in Buenos Aires in 1925. The full congress continues to meet formally every four years.

Great Texas Balloon Race

Competitive hot-air ballooning has soared in popularity since the 1960s, with much of the activity in the United States to be found in the Southwest. Several hot-air balloon events are held annually in Texas, but Longview's Great Texas Balloon Race is the oldest and largest in the state.

Almost 100 competitors from throughout the U.S. and abroad gather at Longview's Gregg County Airport every July, and the three-day event attracts as many as 50,000 visitors. The weekend event also features aircraft and classic car displays, concerts, an arts and crafts show and special activities for children.

Sponsors offer up to $80,000 in prizes for speed and accuracy, testing balloonists' navigational skills. There is also a contest for special shapes in which balloons fashioned like peanuts, rabbits, frankfurters and piggy banks compete.

Weather permitting, balloon ascensions are offered twice daily to paying passengers year-round.

Confederate Reunion Grounds

Despite the bloody strife of the Civil War and numerous hardships forced upon them during Reconstruction, Texans who served the Confederacy in that conflict retained a strong sense of brotherhood throughout their lives.

Starting in 1889, they gathered annually with few interruptions for fifty-seven years at their own campground beside the Navasota River in Limestone County in late July or early August. As many as 5,000 veterans, family members and friends attended in peak years, many arriving on special trains from Dallas, Fort Worth, Houston and other cities.

The Confederate Reunion Grounds State Historical Park expanded from an original twenty acres in 1890 to almost seventy-nine acres in September 1983 when the site was donated by the local post of the United Confederate Veterans to the Texas Parks and Wildlife Department.

Today, it is well maintained by the department, with picnic areas, a playground, fishing in the Navasota River and nature trails in gently rolling oak woodlands.

MIDLAND

Confederate Air Force

Dedicated to preserving World War II aircraft which saw service with all combatants, the Confederate Air Force (CAF) at the international airport in Midland has a fleet of more than 140 aircraft, most in flying condition. It is the world's largest flying museum and was designated as the "official" air force of the State of Texas by the Seventy-first Legislature in 1989.

Its eighty-five-acre complex includes an American Airpower Heritage Museum with an outstanding collection of World War II artifacts, weaponry, uniforms, equipment and aircraft. During the fiftieth anniversary commemoration of World War II (1991-1995), rotating exhibits were changed each year.

The highlight of the year for the "Ghost Squadron" is the second full weekend in October, when its annual air show attracts thousands of visitors. The CAF puts many of its aircraft into the air for re-enactments of World War II battles. The American Airpower Heritage Museum is open to the public every day except Christmas Day and its archives and library are open to historians, students and teachers.

Globe Theatre of the Great Southwest

One of only a few authentic replicas of William Shakespeare's original octagonal theatre outside of England is, surprisingly, in West Texas. Built of wood and plaster, Odessa's Globe Theatre of the Great Southwest, with 410 seats, is naturally on Shakespeare Road on the campus of Odessa College. It is complemented by a nearby replica of Anne Hathaway's cottage, containing Elizabethan furniture and one of the leading Shakespearian libraries in North America.

Since the theatre was completed in 1968, it has hosted an annual Odessa Shakespeare Festival each spring. During the remainder of the year, the theatre presents musicals and concerts.

Shakespeare's original Globe Theatre was built in London in 1598, burned in 1613, was reconstructed and leveled again in 1643 by Puritan extremists.

PALESTINE
National Scientific Balloon Facility

Originally established at Boulder, Colorado, in 1961, the National Scientific Balloon Facility was transferred to Palestine in January 1973. During more that thirty years of operation, it has launched over 1,700 balloons for thirty-five universities, twenty-three other research agencies and thirty-three foreign organizations. The facility is sponsored by the National Aeronautics and Space Administration and operated under contract by New Mexico State University.

The launch area at Palestine not only permits the use of larger balloons with greater payloads, but its two areas provide capability for simultaneous launches during good weather. During its thirty-year history, average payload weight has increased from 407 pounds to more than 3,000 pounds; 5,000-pound payloads to study cosmic rays, micrometeorite activity, and gamma ray and ultraviolet astronomy are common.

Group tours of the facility may be arranged in advance with the resident NASA public affairs officer.

RICHARDSON
History of Aviation Collection

The History of Aviation Collection on the campus of the University of Texas at Dallas is more accurately a composite of more than 200 collections covering every facet of aviation and space history. Established in 1963, it has become one of the foremost such centers in North America. The collection's over 2,500,000 items include 20,000 books, 200,000 journals and 250,000 photographs.

Major collections include the General James H. Doolittle Military Aviation Library, an entire room devoted to Vice Admiral Charles E. Rosendahl of Cleburne, Texas, who was one of the nation's leading proponents of lighter-than-air aviation, and the D. Harold Byrd Business Aviation History Research Center.

Other artifacts and original documents found in the collection relate to other aviation pioneers such as Octave Chanute, Charles A. Lindbergh, Glenn Curtiss, Amelia Earhart and Santos Dumont, as well as present-day Texas-born astronauts.

ROCKSPRINGS
Angora Goat Breeders Museum

Originally from central Turkey, Angora goats have adapted particularly well to only two other places, southern Africa and south Texas. The first few Angoras to arrive in the United States were imported to South Carolina with little success, but a much larger shipment of 150 Angoras was brought to the Southwest in 1867 and has thrived since.

Today, there are 1,560,000 Angora goats in Texas. They yield 14,200,000 pounds of mohair a year with a market value of $12,354,000. Texas mohair production represents ninety percent of that produced in the United States and fully half of all mohair production worldwide.

The story of Angora goats, mohair and their role in the Texas economy is told in a small museum, maintained by the Angora Goat Breeders Association on Austin Street in Rocksprings. It's open to the public Monday, Wednesday and Friday from 9 a.m. to 4 p.m.

National headquarters of the Mohair Council of America is located in San Angelo, with a branch office in New York City for the promotion of mohair.

SAN ANGELO
The Buffalo Soldiers

Fort Concho was established in December 1867 on the site of a former Comanche watering place and remained an active army post until considered no longer needed in 1889. During those twenty-two years, it played a major role in the Indian wars in Texas and served as headquarters for the U.S. Army's all-black troopers of the Ninth and Tenth Cavalry, nicknamed by their Indian adversaries "buffalo soldiers" because their hair was thought to resemble the coat of a buffalo. The troopers weren't offended. In fact, they were so proud of the appellation the Tenth Cavalry added a buffalo to their regimental emblem.

For a generation after the Civil War, black cavalrymen served continuously on the frontier with dedication and courage, exploring unknown territory, building new forts and protecting settlers. From the sweltering Big Bend area of Texas to the Dakotas, they battled Indians, robbers, cattle rustlers, outlaw gunmen and Mexican bandits. They were proud and professional, some of the finest soldiers ever to serve their country.

Hertzberg Circus Museum

The thrill of the Big Top on San Antonio's River Walk? It's the Hertzberg Circus Museum, originally a private collection but operated as a division of the city's public library system since 1942. It was bequeathed to the city by Harry Hertzberg, San Antonio civic leader and state senator.

Its 1930s art deco building houses more than 20,000 artifacts, prints, memorabilia, posters, lithographs, sheet music, handbills, recordings, books, magazines and tapes. It is the oldest such public collection and second largest in the country, attracting more than 45,000 visitors each year.

The museum includes a separate children's section, and special programs, such as storytelling, puppet shows, clowns and magicians, are offered year-round.

Hertzberg was also a collector of rare books, hence the building contains some 15,000 volumes on art, religion, history, costumes and biography, including leaves from illustrated manuscripts. The museum is open six days a week from 10 A.M. to 5 P.M. and on Sunday afternoons during the summer months.

Airborne units spearhead attacks, 1944

TERRELL

Silent Wings Museum

For most of the 6,000 American glider pilots who were trained to land their Waco CG-4A craft in enemy territory during World War II, it was, indeed, a one-way trip. Their flimsy aircraft, constructed of a steel frame, plywood and fabric, had to be towed by C-47 transports to release points in Italy, Normandy, Provence, Holland, Belgium and Burma.

Each glider carried its own weight: thirteen soldiers; a jeep and six soldiers; a small bulldozer and three men; or a 75mm howitzer, five men and eighteen shells. Five hundred CG-4A gliders were dropped into France during the Normandy invasion. Another 100 resupplied the surrounded 101st Airborne Division at Bastogne December 26 - 27, 1944, despite devastating ground fire and a thirty-five percent casualty rate.

The heroism of members of the Glider Pilots Association is preserved in their own museum in Terrell, twenty-seven miles east of Dallas. The Silent Wings Museum tells their story, its centerpiece one of the few Waco CG-4A gliders preserved of some 14,000 built during World War II.

TYLER
Texas Rose Festival

With one-fifth of all the commercial rose bushes produced in the United States coming from Smith County, it's no wonder Tyler is widely known as the "rose capital of the nation."

The city takes its role seriously. It has a municipal rose garden which blooms with 30,000 bushes exhibiting over 400 varieties each year. Close to 100,000 visitors come each year between late May and the first frost. Nearby, a 30,000 square-foot rose garden center houses the Tyler Rose Museum and Texas Rose Research Foundation, as well as conference facilities and a gift shop.

Mid-October is a special time with an annual four-day Texas Rose Festival, featuring a city-wide garden party for residents and visitors in honor of the festival queen.

Computer technology has been used to compile a catalogue which displays color photographs and brief descriptions of 250 rose varieties.

Greer Garson Theatre

The Meadows School of the Arts on the campus of Southern Methodist University offers one of the finest theatre programs in the Southwest. It's been enhanced since September 1992 with the addition of the Greer Garson Theatre, named for the Academy Award-winning actress and longtime Dallas resident. The building also houses the Southwest Film/Video Archives, one of the largest such collections in the United States.

Miss Garson received her Academy Award for her performance in *Mrs. Miniver*. Her other memorable roles included *Goodbye, Mr. Chips, Pride and Prejudice, Random Harvest* and *Sunrise at Campobello*. She appeared in a total of twenty-five films. She was married to the late Colonel E.E. "Buddy" Fogelson, a Texas oilman and philanthropist.

The Greer Garson Theatre covers 50,000 square feet on five levels with an auditorium seating 386. It combines traditional stage design with state-of-the-art technical features.

February 14 Is a Special Day

Valentine may have a population of only 240 souls, but on one day each year, close to 20,000 pieces of outgoing mail are dispatched throughout the United States and to many foreign countries. Each bears a special postmark and a cachet, for the date is February 14, Valentine's Day.

The community, which uses the ZIP code 79854, is situated in Jeff Davis County astride Route 90 at the foot of the Davis Mountains. It's halfway between Marfa and Van Horn. Legend has it the community was named by a crew laying track for the Texas and New Orleans Railway Company when they reached that location on Valentine's Day, 1882.

People send their Valentine's Day cards for special handling, often bearing stamps which express their affection. Since the United States Postal Service issued its first stamp inscribed with the word LOVE in January 1973, more than a dozen such stamps have been issued.

BIBLIOGRAPHY

Allen, Edward. *Heroes of Texas*. New York: Simon & Schuster, Inc., 1970.

Almanac of Famous People. Detroit: Gale Research, Inc., 1994.

Alter, Judy, *The Comanches*. New York: Franklin Watts, 1994.

Astronaut Fact Book. Houston: National Aeronautics and Space Administration, 1993.

Baker, T. Lindsey. *The Polish Texans*. San Antonio: Institute of Texan Cultures, University of Texas, 1982.

Cartwright, Gary. *Galveston: A History of The Island*. New York: Atheneum, 1991.

Churchill, James E. *The Olympic Story*. Danbury: Grolier Incorporated, 1979.

Clarke, Donald. *The Encyclopedia of Popular Music*. New York: Viking Penguin, Inc., 1989.

Connor, Seymour V., et al. *Battles of Texas*. Waco: Texian Press, 1967.

——————— . *Texas, A History*. New York: Thomas Y. Crowell Company, 1971.

Couch, Ernie and Jill. *Texas Trivia*. Nashville: Rutledge Hill Press, 1991.

Darby, Jean. *Eisenhower: A Man Called Ike*. Minneapolis: Lerner Publications, 1989.

Davis, John L. *The Danish Texans*. San Antonio: Institute of Texan Cultures, University of Texas, 1979.

Davis, Joe Tom. *Legendary Texians*. Austin: Eakin Press, 1982.

Dingus, Anne. *Dictionary of Texas Misinformation*. Austin: Texas Monthly Press, 1987.

——————— . *The Book of Texas Lists*. Austin: Texas Monthly Press, 1981.

Encyclopedia Americana, Danbury: Grolier Incorporated, 1990.

Fehrenbach, T. R. *Lone Star*. New York: American Legacy Press, 1981.

Gard, Wayne. *The Chisholm Trail*. Norman: University of Oklahoma Press, 1954.

Goldberg, Alfred. *History of The United States Air Force*. Princeton: Van Nostrand Company, 1957.

Greene, A. C. *900 Miles on The Butterfield Trail*. Denton: University of North Texas Press, 1994.

—————. *Texas Sketches*. Dallas: Taylor Publishing Company, 1985.

Haley, J. Evetts. *Charles Goodnight: Cowman and Plainsman*. Norman: University of Oklahoma Press, 1949.

—————. *Texas, An Album of History*. New York: Doubleday & Company, 1985.

Hall, Kermit L. *Oxford Companion to The Supreme Court of The United States*. New York: Oxford University Press, 1992.

Halliwell, Leslie. *Filmgoer's Companion*. New York: Charles Scribner's Sons, 1988.

Hanes, Bailey C. *Bill Pickett, Bulldogger*. Norman: University of Oklahoma Press, 1977.

Hickock, Ralph. *Who's Who of Sports Champions*. Boston: Houghton Mifflin Company, 1995.

—————. *Who Was Who in American Sports*. New York: Hawthorn Books, 1971.

Holmes, Jon. *Texas, A Self-Portrait*. New York: Harry N. Abrams, Inc., 1983.

Hood, Joseph F. *When Monsters Roamed The Skies: The Saga of The Dirigible Airship*. New York: Grosset & Dunlap, 1968.

Insight Guides, Texas. Boston: Houghton Mifflin Company, 1993.

Johnson, Cecil. *Guts: Legendary Black Cowboy Bill Pickett*. Fort Worth: Summit Group, 1994.

Johnston, Leah Carter. *San Antonio*. San Antonio: The Naylor Company, 1976.

Karst, Gene. *Who's Who in Professional Baseball*. New Rochelle: Arlington Press, 1973.

Lavender, David. *The Great West*. New York: American Heritage, 1965.

Leachman, William D. *Helium*. Washington: U.S. Department of The Interior, 1994.

Leckie, William H. *The Buffalo Soldiers*. Norman: University of Oklahoma Press, 1967.

Maguire, Jack. *Texas, Amazing But True*. Austin: Eakin Press, 1984.

McComb, David G. *Texas, A Modern History*. Austin: University of Texas Press, 1989.

McDonald, Archie P. *Texas, All Hail The Mighty State*. Austin: Eakin Press, 1983.

—————. *Texas: What Do You Know About The Lone Star State?* Fort Worth: TCU Press, 1993.

Mallon, Bill. *Quest for Gold*. New York: Leisure Press, 1984.

Mayfield, John S. *Sidney Lanier in Texas*. Dallas: Boyd Press, 1912.

Miller, Jay, and Roger Bilstein. *Aviation in Texas*. Austin: Texas Monthly Press, 1985.

Miller, Nathan. *Theodore Roosevelt, A Life*. New York: William Morrow & Company, 1992.

Miller, Ray. *Texas Parks, A History and Guide*. Houston: Cordovan Press, 1984.

————. *Texas Forts, A History and Guide*. Houston: Cordovan Press, 1985.

Morison, Samuel Eliot. *The European Discovery of America*. New York: Oxford University Press, 1974.

Murphy, Edward F. *Heroes of World War II*. Novato, California: Presidio Press, 1990.

Nevin, David. *The Texans*. Alexandria: Time-Life Books, 1975.

New Handbook of Texas, Ron Tyler, *et al.*, eds. Austin: Texas State Historical Association, 1996.

O'Rear, Sybil. *Charles Goodnight: Pioneer Cowman*. Austin: Eakin Press, 1990.

Perret, Geoffrey. *There's A War To Be Won*. New York: Random House, Inc., 1991.

Place, Marian T. *Comanches and Other Indians of Texas*. New York: Harcourt, Brace & World, 1970.

Reichstein, Andreas V. *Rise of The Lone Star*. College Station: Texas A&M University Press, 1989.

Roosevelt, Theodore. *The Rough Riders*. New York: New American Library, 1961.

Ruff, Ann. *Amazing Texas Monuments and Museums*. Houston: Gulf Publishing Company, 1984.

Scott, Robert L., Jr. *Flying Tiger, Chennault of China*. New York: Doubleday & Company, 1959.

Sperry, Neil. *Complete Guide to Texas Gardening*. Dallas: Taylor Publishing Company, 1982.

Standard Postage Stamp Catalogue. Sidney: Scott Publishing Company, 1995.

Stein, R. Conrad. *The Lone Star Republic*. Chicago: Regensteiner Publishing Enterprises, 1988.

Supreme Court of the United States. Washington: Commission on the Bicentennial of the United States Constitution, 1992.

Talley, Mike. *Texas State Travel Guide*. Austin: Texas Department of
Transportation, 1995.

Thomas, Richard Louis. *Who's Who on United States*. Sidney: Amos
Press, 1991.

Tyler, Paula Eyrich and Ron C. *Texas Museums: A Guidebook*. Austin:
University of Texas Press, 1983.

Wallis, George A. *Cattle Kings of The Staked Plains*. Denver: Sage
Books, 1964.

Weber, David J. *The Spanish Frontier in North America*. New Haven:
Yale University Press, 1992.

Webster's American Military Biographies. Springfield: G.C. Merriam
Company, 1978.

Welch, June Rayfield. *The Glory That Was Texas*. Dallas: GLA Press,
1975.

————. *Historic Sites of Texas*. Dallas: Yellow Rose Press, 1992.

Whisenhunt, Donald W. *Chronology of Texas History*. Austin: Eakin
Press, 1982.

————. *Texas, A Sesquicentennial Celebration*. Austin: Eakin Press,
1984.

INDEX